If You Don't Have a Plan, Stay in the Car

Mack Hanan

amacom

American Management Association

Reprinted by permission from Sales and Marketing Management magazine.

Library of Congress Cataloging-in-Publication Data

Hanan, Mack.
   If you don't have a plan, stay in the car.

   1. Selling. 2. Profit. I. American Management
Association. II. Title.
HF438.25.H347   1987   658.8'1   87-47706
ISBN 0-8144-5936-6

Printing number

10 9 8 7 6 5 4 3 2 1

Preface

This is a book of sales dialogues about improving customer profits. Every sales representative, manager, and customer who speaks here is talking about profits. The customers want more of them and they want them faster. The sales representatives and their managers want to supply them because they know that customer profits are the base—the cause, really—of their own profits from sales. Whenever any two or more of these key players come into contact with one another, they begin a profit dialogue.

In this way, each of the players talks about adding value. Sales representatives and their managers add value in the form of higher profits to their customers' businesses. Customers return some of this added value in the form of higher margins to their suppliers. Both win. Both grow. Both create the kind of relationship that allows them to win and win again, a partnership in profit improvement.

In each dialogue in this book, partners talk about improving their mutual profits. They come at it from many different angles. They often take divergent positions about how it can best be done. They confront one another and ruffle one another's preconceptions, sometimes taking the long way around and other times grossly oversimplifying. They twit each other, turn phrases to their advantage, and play hardball. All the while, they are selling. If the way they go about it seems perfectly natural, that's because it is. Every dialogue in this book is real, both in its original incarnation and the interactions among the people involved. I have lent my ear and my pen to record them. They have written themselves.

Selling, no matter who sells what to whom, operates in only one way: by dialogue. Sales representatives sell by talking. They talk to

their managers. They talk to their customers. Managers and customers talk back. When representatives rehearse a sale, they even talk
to themselves and, by role-playing the customer, they talk from both
sides of their mouths.

The sales representative who has nothing to say has nothing to
sell. The sales representative who has no one to talk to has no one to
sell to. No matter what the product or service, no matter who the
market, every sale is based on the same basic discourse: why my
product or service offers you more value than either a competitive
product or your own solution that you are using now. Selling is
impossible without comparison. And comparison is impossible
without dialogue.

Sales dialogue is therefore a dissertation on comparative values.

Old-fashioned and now obsolete sales talk used to concentrate
on proving that one product's features and benefits were better than
another's. Modern sales talk proves how the customer will be
better—how much less costly an office or factory operation will be,
how much more productively its workforce will function, or how
many more sales dollars will be earned. These are the only things
worth talking about because these are the only things—costs, productivity, and sales—that can improve customer profits. And customer profits are the only thing that customers can never have
enough of and are always open to buy.

Over the past 20 years, I have counselled tens of thousands of
sales representatives and their managers in the strategies of improving customer profits. In the course of our dialogue—where we were
comparing profit-improvement selling strategies against old-fashioned selling of features and benefits—we have traded experiences as
well as philosophies. I tell them *how:* how to sell improved profits.
They tell me *what:* what it is like for them to do so, what it sounds
like and feels like to act as a profit partner, what problems they must
overcome, and what solutions they apply.

Inevitably, this is a book of solutions. A sales manager solves a
representative's problem. A representative solves a customer's problem. A customer solves a problem for all three of them. Sometimes
the tables are turned and a representative solves a problem for a
manager. Each solution is a model. It is a model of what works.
Therefore it can be learned from.

Each solution is also a model of some of the most laudable qualities in the sales process: persistence in the face of repeated frustrations, ingenuity in dealing with the traditional pressures and constraints of "not invented here" and "don't fix it if it ain't broke," and dedication to enrich the customer-supplier partnership with measurable new values.

If you are a sales representative, these things are worth talking about with your manager. If you are a manager, these things are worth talking about with your representatives. Both of you will find these things worth talking about with your customers. They will make more money for you than anything else you can think of to say.

A Word to Women Who Sell

The sales representatives and managers whose dialogues are recorded in this book are predominantly men. This is because selling, along with most business functions, is predominantly male-oriented, and so it is only natural that this small work of art imitates life. Although this is the way of the real world, the world is changing. And although women are vastly outnumbered in sales, their quality is outstanding. In every sales force I know, women are always among the top producers. They persist in adversity; they partner with men and women customers alike; they pursue opportunity, track it down and capture it with a grace and precision that is often denied to the natural capacities of men. As consultative sellers, the best women are unmatchable. They are represented by Linda in this book and will, I hope, find many more models of themselves in the next collection of these dialogues.

Mack Hanan

This book is dedicated to
Robert H. Albert,
who made it possible for
these dialogues on sales strategies
to make their initial appearance
in *Sales and Marketing Management*
magazine, and for their author
to share a uniquely rewarding
partnership with him and his people
for many, and yet too few, years.

Contents

If You're Looking for the Easy Way to Sell, Stop Now—It's the Hard Way

"If you propose to teach our sales managers how to do their jobs better," the president says to me, "then you must know something they don't know. Is that a correct assumption?"

"Not quite," I answer. "I might be able to teach them how to apply their knowledge better, but I really can't say I know anything they don't. As a matter of fact, in the past decade or so, I think I've learned only three things about sales management."

"It took you ten years to learn just three things!" the president exclaims. "At that rate, I would expect them to be gems. Are they?"

I decide to let him be the judge, and so I start off by saying, "The most important thing I've learned is that selling a man something means doing something for him. Not just describing benefits but delivering them. In fact, the word I've come to like best is *installing:* taking out your screwdriver and pliers and actually meshing the operating benefit with one of your customer's key processes. This means you don't just take the order; you don't just oversee delivery; you don't just handle complaints. You accept responsibility for *making the benefit happen* in the customer's plant. Most important, you make sure the customer realizes he is better off, not because of the benefit per se, but because of *you.*

"This is more than benefit selling. I call it 'benefit installing.' It puts enormous pressure on the salesman because it makes an applications engineer out of him. The salesman who likes to call himself a 'problem solver' has to put his time and talent where his mouth is. The problem, whatever it is, can't be considered solved until the benefit is installed and is delivering on a continuous basis as a result of the salesman's efforts. If a sales manager is serious about having his men add value for his customers, this is the only way I know that it can be done."

1

"So your first piece of knowledge," the president sums up, "is that the salesman has to roll up his sleeves and get his hands dirty installing benefits in customer processes. Does your second fact take off from this idea?"

"Very much so. Because as soon as you talk of adding value, the question arises, What is the nature of the value to be added? A lot of people believe in the gospel of multiple benefits—'My product gives you these seven benefits and his gives you only five.' It took me a long while to realize it, but these bells and whistles are really only what I call contributory benefits. There's only one major value, profit improvement, which I regard as the ultimate benefit. I like to see a sales force out selling the added value of improved profit a customer can expect when he lets the sales force install benefits. The added value then becomes quantified. It has a number and becomes a tangible value that can be bottom-lined and put in the bank." I surveyed my one-man audience, expecting a sharp reaction.

"That's all very well and good," the president says. "But how do you propose to put numbers on profit improvement when it's the customer's profit that you're trying to improve? How do you get *his* numbers, which you need before you can promise to improve them?"

"The answer to that is the third thing I've learned: The only way you can do it is to develop partnerships in profit improvement with your customers."

"Great idea!" the president scoffs. "My salespeople are going around our marketplace, sleeves rolled up, to install benefits and promising the added value of improved profit. Now you say they have to create a sort of industrial buddy system with our customers. It's hard enough to *sell* them. How can we think in terms of partnership?"

"It's probably the most difficult of the three things to do," I agree. "In fact, it's so difficult that if your salespeople can learn to do it, they can have a lock on their customer relationships that will be hard for any competitor to break.

"The key idea is understanding what makes a partnership. I used to think that it was the size of the promise—the bigger the promise, the more vibrant the partnership. Then I wondered if it might not be the creative brilliance of the salesman's proposals that gave a customer ideas he could get nowhere else.

"But I found that big promises aroused more suspicion than fellowship and that brilliant ideas were usually valued at a dime a dozen. Now I think I've learned the true basis for partnership, which is simple: To have a partner, you first have to be one. And the way to be one is to make it comfortable for the other man to share your objective of improved profit.

"The device that enables him to feel secure enough to come aboard with you is the control procedures you set up to do two things. First, you must avoid the unthinkable risk of catastrophic failure; the customer must know that the salesman has a system to prevent the two of them from going down the tube together. Second, control. It's mandatory to have a series of early-warning checkpoints that the salesman and his customer can both monitor to make sure that the installed benefits are happening and that the improved profit is being generated. Without controls against failure, there can never be a partnership."

"So," says the president, "these are the three things you carry around in your head about the sales function: Install benefits, improve profit, and set up a control system that makes the customer comfortable and secure in working with you. Three things, that's all. And it's taken you ten years to learn them. Would you mind telling me why? Is it because they're so obvious?"

"No," I say defensively, "I don't think they're obvious at all. Maybe now, but not before."

"All right, let me guess again. Did it take you ten years because you started out with a long list and, by process of elimination, had to separate the wheat from the chaff?"

"No, I didn't have a long list to start from. I had to build my own. In ten years, these are the three things I've been able to put on it."

"Well, then, why *did* it take so long?"

"I think it's because I looked first for the easy ways. I found lots of them—the long list you spoke of. They had one problem: They didn't bring home consistently superior profitable sales volume. Then I changed my approach. I looked for the hard ways, most of which had to do with customer processes. When I found them, I resisted them; they were hard to learn and even harder to teach. Once I stopped resisting them and started studying them, it all straightened out."

For the first time in our conversation, the president seems to be convinced of something, though I'm not sure what. I'm surprised when he finally says, "It sounds to me as though what you just said is the fourth thing you have learned in ten years. From my standpoint, it's the most important selling idea of all."

1
Penetration Planning

Getting the Right Foot in the Right Door

If You Don't Have a Plan, Stay in the Car

"We're here," the sales representative says to his manager, who has come along with him on the call. The young man turns off the engine and waits for the manager to get out, but he just sits there.

"Where's *here?*" the manager asks.

"Right on the other side of this parking lot is one of my key accounts, maybe the most important. I told you back at the office. Don't you remember?"

"That's not what I'm asking," the manager interrupts. "What I meant by *here* wasn't the name of the account. It was the name of the problem."

"What problem?" the representative asks.

"The problem you've come here to solve. What is it? What are you going to do about it?"

"I don't know about any problem," the representative answers. "As far as I know, everything is all right with this customer."

"So," says the manager, "we find ourselves sitting in front of the eighth wonder of the world: a multimillion-dollar piece of business, one of the largest companies in its industry, and it doesn't have a single problem."

"None that I know of," says the representative.

"That's what I was afraid of."

The sales representative, like so many others, feels he can defend to the death his right to make a call on a customer with no specific problem in mind. His manager, like an increasing number of sales supervisors these days, is equally committed to the opposite point of view.

"You mean you don't want me ever to make a call on a customer unless I know in advance that he has a problem I can solve?" the representative asks.

"Unless it's your father's company," replies the manager.

"Well, are we going to go in or aren't we?" the representative wants to know.

7

"As soon as you tell me where *in* is, I'll let you know," the manager says. "Tell me where you'd be taking me, to what part of the customer's business. Who are the decision makers, and what problems do they have that you can solve? If you can't answer those questions, we'll end up with the purchasing agent and you'll be asking him if there's anything he wants to buy today. I can't *afford* you, if that's the way you're going to spend your time."

"But how can I know what problems a customer has unless I call on him first and get him talking to me?"

"That depends on who the *him* is, doesn't it?" the manager says. "The answer to that is the same as to where *in* is and what you mean by *here*. That's where you learn customer problems, not in purchasing where the problems are price, price, and more price, with maybe a delivery or two thrown in for good measure. What can you learn from that?"

"That our prices are too high, for one thing," the representative replies.

"Or, to say the same thing more accurately," the manager shoots back, "that our knowledge of customer problems and how to solve them is too low to support our price."

"So how long are we going to sit here?" the representative wants to know.

"Until you come up with a problem you can solve—or 5:00 p.m.—whichever comes first."

Some time later inside the plant, the manufacturing vice president of the customer company is frowning at his secretary's message. "Suppliers? What do they want to see me for? If they want to solve one of our downtime problems, see if Ed will see them. If they really have anything to offer, Ed will get back to me on it."

The resulting call is not ideal, perhaps, but it accomplishes more than calling on a purchasing agent. "We do a lot of business in your industry," the representative tells Ed as they sit down in his office. "We've learned how your lines must operate to keep costs down. We're familiar with the way downtime adds to your costs and what each day you're down does to margins here at the plant. We have a solution that can keep you operating longer. That's why we came by."

"We nearly didn't," the manager says. "We almost skipped you."

"Why would you do that?" Ed asks. "Aren't we important?"

"That's just it," says the manager. "You're so important to us that we wanted to make sure of our facts and figures before we asked for your time. But we're taking the chance that we can interest you so that you'll let us come back with a proposal with which we can show you how much we can save you."

"My door is open," Ed says.

Back in the car, the manager makes his point to the representative. "That's where *here* is," he says. "That's where you go *in*. That's who's *in charge*. Are you glad we took the two hours out in the parking lot to thrash it out?"

"We found a problem, that's for sure," says the representative. "It was exciting to talk to the man who actually has the problem and who can do something about solving it. But wasn't it embarrassing to have to talk only in generalities and not leave him anything specific he could take action on?"

The manager agrees. "Yes, it was embarrassing. We can't let it happen again. But it wasn't as embarrassing as walking in here without a hint of a problem to solve."

The representative gets the point and adds, "We can't let that happen again, either."

Making a Customer Our National Account Means Nothing Unless We Make Ourselves His National Supplier

"It was the last thing I ever expected," the salesperson says to his manager. "I walked in there all charged up, just like you'd told me, and I laid it right on him: 'Smile,' I said. 'We've chosen you to be one of our most valued customers, a national account.' Whammo! That's as far as I got."

"Do you remember his exact words?" the manager asks.

"Remember? I'll never forget them. He told me, 'You think we're going to roll over on our backs with our legs in the air because your company, in its great wisdom, has chosen us to be one of your national accounts? I'm sorry to disappoint you. In the first place, we're *everybody's* national account, so the distinction, if there ever was any, wore off a long time ago. But, more important, no supplier can just walk in here and tell us we've made his club, especially when we never applied for it in the first place.'"

"It seems to me," the manager says, "that he was challenging you to tell him the benefits of being our national account. Didn't you interpret it that way?"

"I never had the chance. The next thing he said—and it was the last thing—was that if we really wanted him to be a national account, we'd have to *earn it first*. He really emphasized the last three words."

"Earn it first?" repeats the manager. "I wonder what he meant by that."

"I do, too," says the salesperson matter-of-factly.

National accounts, whether they're called by that name or key accounts, major accounts, or target accounts, are every supplier's main market. They're the 20% or fewer of all customers that can contribute as much as 80% or more of all profitable sales volume.

They're the heart and soul of a supplier's business. A top sales executive cannot afford to neglect any one of them. To do so means leaving customer needs exposed to competition. Nor can a supplier afford to lose a key account. No amount of other business can make up for the loss of future revenues and earnings, to say nothing of present sales.

These are the principal reasons why key accounts are vital to suppliers. But what's in it for the customer? Why would a customer get uppity and tell an enthusiastic supplier thanks, but no thanks, for the chance to be one of his national accounts?

A few days later, the salesperson and the manager make a joint call on the customer. "Our account manager tells me you said we'd have to earn the right to name you a national account," the sales manager says. "Neither of us understood what you meant, so I thought we'd drop by and see if you could enlighten us. What do you mean by earning our way? We thought it was our role to qualify you and not the other way around."

"That just the problem," the customer says. "You can't imagine what it's like to have practically every supplier we do business with— and a lot that we don't—come in here and say the exact same thing: 'You've won the lottery! Here's your badge. Wear it, and that will give us the right to sell you up, down, and sideways.' That's why I told your man that if you want a special relationship with us, you have to earn it."

"We've always believed in doing just that," the manager says. "We're a quality house from A to Z. We have quality-controlled products, dependable service, knowledgeable people, and fair prices. We think we earn our wings every day."

"So do your competitors," the customer says. "Do you come in here in any way different from them? Of course not. Do their products lack quality? Is their service undependable? Are their people ignorant or their prices unfair? Really, your differences earn you only the right to be just like them, nobody special. If we're going to be your national account and you, as a result, are going to be our national supplier, you're going to have to do better than that. When you think you can, let us hear from you."

Almost a month later, the manager and salesperson sit across from the customer again. This time, the salesperson does the talking:

"We've been spending the past few weeks working hard to learn how we could earn the right to call you a national account," he says. "We've been reviewing the costs in your operations that we believe we can reduce, and we've calculated the dollars we can save you. We've also been looking at your sales, asking ourselves how we can help you increase them. You'll see the calculations we've made about the dollars we can add that way.

"What we've done is combine these two approaches in a plan to improve your profits as a result of working with us in an intensive, comprehensive manner. If you work with us this way, you'll be what we call a national account. But more important to you is what you'll be as a business: You'll be more productive, in more control of your costs, more competitive, and, on the bottom line, more profitable.

"Making you these things is our way of acknowledging your importance to us. It's our best shot at earning the right to be chosen by you as a supplier, for you to work with us just as intensively as we'll work with you."

"That's a lot better than what you said the first time," the customer says. "All right, now I'm ready to have you pin the badge on me."

"At the proper time, we'll be glad to do that," the salesperson says. "First, you have to earn it."

Just When You Think You've Got the Customer All Tied Up, He May Have You on a String

The sales representative can't wait to break the news to his manager. "They're going to go with us exclusively," he says. "We are their single source for the entire run—their dedicated supplier, they call it—so I guess that means we've got them, doesn't it?"

The manager frowns. "What do you think: Do we have them or do they have us?"

More and more companies are moving to single sources of supply in many areas of their purchasing. The old rule of never depending on only one supplier is being overtaken by the realities of the 1980s. The need for quality control has superseded the need for safety.

A single source that has been given all the business is thought to have a greater reason to press for zero defects, as well as more resources to carry out such a program, than either of two suppliers that share, say, 40% or 50% of an order. At the same time, a single source can be asked to provide extra services for a customer in return for its extra revenues. It can furnish warehousing and accommodate inventory, taking both of these costs off a customer's hands. It can operate on a just-in-time delivery system by making many small, frequent shipments exactly when they are needed. It may even build a plant or warehouse next door.

It is also expected that a one-source supplier will be increasingly accommodating on its price. "How large a first run do we have with them?" the manager asks. "At what price?"

It is typically a moderate run at a reasonable margin—not a bonanza but not a bloodbath either. "Let me role-play the customer with you," the manager says. "We're coming to the end of the run,

O.K.? Now let me ask you a few questions. What's it been like for your company doing this job for us?"

"Great," the sales representative replies.

"Everybody happy over at your place?"

"Sure. It's been a good relationship all around. You're our kind of people. As a matter of fact, some of our folks say they wish all our customers would work with us this way."

"Sounds like you might want to go around a second time with us, then, if I hear right."

"You hear me," says the representative. "This time around we'll do even better for you."

"Oh," says the manager, still role-playing the customer, "how's that?"

"Well, you know that when you start an initial order like yours, there are always some inefficiencies on any supplier's part until he gets rolling. We've smoothed those out now. We've got our process down pat. We've got the demand-delivery system running smoothly now, almost to the point where you can set your watch by it. And our people have learned how yours like to operate, so they can give you what you want, not only in the product but in the ways we service you."

"I would expect, then, that all these efficiencies can be translated into lower costs for a second run," says the manager. "In that case, I'd also expect you can do better on your price."

"Oh, oh," says the representative. "I walked right into that one, didn't I?"

Making price concessions in order to retain the position of sole source is not an issue that can be walked *away* from. Sometimes the margin squeeze takes place up front at the time a supplier is likely to be excited about getting a lock on a volume order. Otherwise it happens at reorder time when the supplier makes his bid to continue.

"Think of where we are at precisely this point in our negotiation," the sales manager says. "You have 80% or more of our capacity tied up with one customer. All our machinery is dedicated to his exact specifications, no one else's. There is no one else because we haven't been able to cultivate any other customer. How would we supply them?"

"But we'd have the volume of several customers, wouldn't we?"

says the representative. "And, don't forget, it would be a sure thing. That's got to be worth something."

"Yes, it is," says the manager. "But is it worth our profit? And not just short-term, either. Think of something else. If we hitch our wagon to one customer, we're betting that he will be the successful entry in his own markets, or at least one of the winners. If we're wrong, we have everything to lose. Someone else will be supplying the leaders. Even if we're right, he will be looking to us for successive price breaks, more free services, and greater investments on our part."

"So what should I do?" the representative asks. "Tell them thanks but no thanks?"

"Tell them thanks and then get to work. Your job has just begun. First, go to work with the customer. Sit down with him and a couple of financial people, his and ours, and work out a *long-term* mutual profit plan for both of us doing business together. Tell them we and they must profit together or we won't have a customer and they won't have a supplier. After all, the reason they picked us suggests that they value us, so they have a stake in keeping us healthy."

The representative thinks for a moment. "That way, you want to show them how much they're getting from us in the way of cost savings and investment and how our price must reflect that, right?"

"Right," the manager says. "Then I want you to sit down with our R&D people and theirs and plan progressive innovations that we can bring to their product over the next 18 months or so—along with what we're going to have to do with our own engineering and manufacturing to make sure that we remain the leading-edge supplier. If we stay ahead technologically, we won't have any problem convincing the customer that we have a reason for keeping our margins high."

"You know," the representative says, "all that sounds good sitting here in the office but . . . I don't know."

"Why won't it sound just as good sitting in the customer's office?"

"Suppose it doesn't, then what?"

"Then I guess you'll just have to excuse yourself and get up to go out and sell."

Stay Out of the Middle of the Market—There's No Room There to Make Both Ends Meet

If you sell Rolls-Royces, you know that the top of the line is moving. So is the bottom, but not the models in the middle. If you sell vacations or rent out vacation homes, the top and the bottom are moving, but not the middle. If you sell diversified lines of industrial equipment, office systems, or even services, the same thing is happening. There is no middle market anymore. Where has it gone?

Some of the former middle market has migrated upward. It pays a little more but requires a much greater benefit, either in product benefits, services, or prestige. Most of the middle market, however, has dropped down, paying less but not, according to its perception of the value-to-price relationship, having to accept fewer benefits. As one customer notes, "Our suppliers keep treating us as if we were still middle-of-the-line buyers. They hope we'll move back up." The raw truth is that for most midmarket customers who have become low-end purchasers, moving back up will never happen.

"If you're in the middle," a sales manager says, "you're in trouble. It is hard to justify the added price. Either you end up giving away products or services so that when the customer compares you with top-of-the-line suppliers, he says, 'What's the advantage?' Or you don't, so that when the customer compares what he gets with the low-end customer, he says, 'What's the advantage?' Whichever way, you lose."

Because the midrange product doesn't seem to have enough added benefit for value-conscious customers and seems to cost too much for price-conscious customers, it is running out of constituency. As a result, markets are polarizing. There is a high end, a low end, and very little in between.

How can sales managers take advantage of their market's two-way split? "I don't think it is a case of one market with two ends," a sales manager says. "I think it's two separate and distinct markets, and we are organizing two sales forces to deal with them. Each has its own customer base; even when the customers are the same company, the decision makers are different. Our offering is different too, in how comprehensive it is, how much service support accompanies it, and, of course, in price. It is a two-tier operation."

The bottom tier is the price tier. Products are sold at this level on price and performance. Because price is low, margins are low too; to make bottom-tier selling profitable, volume must be high. This is the level of commodity selling to mass, undifferentiated markets. It might seem, therefore, that the bottom-tier sales force must be large to ring many doorbells and chase smokestacks. But this would make the cost of sales unrecoverable.

"The bottom-tier staff is actually smaller than the top-tier," the sales manager continues. "Very simply, we can't afford personal selling to low-margin customers. We use direct mail as much as possible. We use telemarketing, calling our repeat customers several times each month. We also try to computerize their ordering from us so that their predictable replacement purchases are handled automatically, untouched by expensive human hands—either theirs or ours. Some of our customers never see a sales representative."

If a bottom-tier customer wants applications help or support services over and above the fundamentals, he is billed for it. When a salesperson calls, it is probably to explore a new opportunity to see if it deserves top-tier service.

The top tier is where the profits are. Accordingly, the top tier is also where comprehensive product systems are sold, comprehensive services are applied, and comprehensive sales force resources can be brought to bear.

In the words of the sales manager, "Whereas a bottom-tier customer may never see our representatives, a top-tier customer sees them all the time. By 'customer,' I am not talking about purchasing agents. They are bottom tier. I mean middle-level managers of the customer business functions that we sell to. We position ourselves as their consultants in improving the profits of those functions, and that means we have to know those operations inside out. Very often, our representatives are actual residents in our key customer businesses. They practically live there, learning their customers' problems and seeing opportunities for our solutions."

At the top tier, sales are based on value rather than price. The customer wants to maximize the value of his profit far more than minimize the cost of his price. He will pay more to gain more as long as what he gains significantly exceeds what he pays. This is return-on-investment selling, where the price of the investment is evaluated according to the size and quickness of the return.

Someone asks the sales manager, "As you analyze your strategy to deal with the disappearance of the middle market, where is selling really concentrated in your organization?"

"Funny thing," the manager replies. "We do very little traditional selling at the bottom tier any more, not in the sense of a representative sitting across from the purchasing agent. That still happens, of course, but maybe less than half as often as it used to. At the top tier we do little traditional selling either. We do research on customer problems, run cost-benefit analyses to calculate the optimal solutions, and then teach the customers' people how to apply the best solution in the most cost-effective way."

"So who's really selling anymore?"

"It's not the bottom-tier sales force. It's not the top. I guess it must be me. I'm selling like crazy to get our people to understand two-tier selling."

When Selling the Customer Is Foremost on Your Mind, You May Never Learn What's Foremost on His

"Your first thought of the day: That's the one crucial to your success," the sales manager is saying. "It sets your mind, targets your motivation. Right from the very moment you open your eyes, even before your feet hit the floor, your entire day can be predetermined by what you think. So that's what I want to know from each of you: your first thought of the day." To start things off, he points to someone in the front row.

"Sales," says the man.

"Sell harder," says a second.

"Sell more creatively," says a woman in the group.

"Does everybody agree?" the manager interrupts. "It's sales, sales, and more sales. The purpose of a sales representative is to sell the customer, then sell him again and again. Let's see hands." All but one goes up.

Since the 1950s, when something called The Total Marketing Concept was in vogue, it has been popular to believe that the purpose of a business is to create customers. It follows that the purpose of the sales function is to sell to more and more prospects as its role in the creation process. True, sales forces inform. They provide service. They entertain. But they must sell if their part in the customer-creation process is to be fulfilled. A customer doesn't become a customer, it has been said many times, until he buys something.

There is just one problem with this kind of thinking: All the others who sell to the customer think the same way. The customer they call "theirs" is everyone else's too. There is no differentiation and thus no basis for preference other than price. Is this the intended meaning of the Total Marketing Concept: selling on an ever-lower price?

"Why aren't you raising your hand?" the manager asks the lone holdout. "Don't you think of sales from the time you get up in the morning until you go to bed?"

"No," says the representative. "It's the *last* thing I think of. I try never to let it enter my mind."

The room becomes hushed. The manager turns red, then blue. "Unless my hearing is impaired, you're saying you don't think of selling the customer. What, then, do you think of?"

"*Not* selling him," the representative says. "I tell myself over and over again before each call, *don't sell him.*"

"That's negative thinking!" the manager shouts. "You just can't tell yourself what not to do. You have to be positive about something if you're ever going to sell. Don't you believe in that?"

"Sure," says the representative. "But first, I have to clear my mind of temptation. After all, I'm a sales representative. The easiest thing in the world is for me to believe I should be selling. Once I remove myself from being tempted, however, I can think more positively about my mission."

"Which is?" the manager asks irritably.

"Which is to help my customer improve his profits. I have to sell him something to do that, of course, but that's just the means. The end is that his profit is improved."

"So when you get up in the morning, your first thought is not to sell but to improve a customer's profit. And you think that's concentrating on the end, not the means. How does that influence what you do from that moment on?"

"It guides everything I do," the representative says. "Since I'm not selling, I don't have to talk about my product. If I don't talk about my product, I don't have to talk about the competition's. Therefore, no one can ask me about price. Right away, I'm differentiating myself from everybody else who calls on that customer."

"What do you talk about? You must say *something.*"

"I talk about him, about where the costs are in his business that I can help reduce, and about where his sales opportunities are that I can help him increase. Those are the ways I'm going to use to improve his profit."

"You turn over the sales call's leadership to the customer?" the manager asks incredulously. "Why do you let him talk to you about his own business when you should be telling him about our capabilities and our systems?"

"Because I once asked myself the same question about my customers that you asked us about ourselves: What's their first thought of the day? I didn't know, so I asked them. They told me it was making money, improving their profits, so I decided I would think the same thing."

"And you find that this works better than selling harder?" the manager asks.

"Right. Because when I show how I can improve a customer's profit, he buys harder. I don't have to sell at all."

The Great Sales Paradox: You Sell a Product, but the Customer Really Buys Its Contribution to Profits

"I hate to tell you this," the customer says. "You've worked hard for the sale, you know your stuff, and you made a good impression on our people. But we're going to give the order to one of your competitors."

In selling, you win some and you lose some. The sales you hate to lose, naturally, are the ones you try hardest to win. Sometimes you can see the justification and sometimes not. No matter what, you have to be a good sport and accept the customer's verdict. Or do you?

In this case, when the sales representative doesn't say anything, the customer quickly adds to his brief announcement. "Rightly or wrongly, some of the people here believe that there's a clear-cut product superiority involved. They've decided to go with the best performance they can get for the buck."

That gives the representative his opening. "You've made a good decision," he says. "Whether it's the best or not, who's to say? But what you did won't hurt you. If the supplier is who I think it is, you will get a product your people can be proud of. Pound for pound, dollar for dollar, I might have made the same decision if I were you."

The customer looks relieved. "That's a very statesmanlike attitude for you to take under the circumstances. Quite frankly, I was a little apprehensive about telling you; I didn't know what your reaction would be, especially after you'd fought so hard to win."

"I'll be frank with you, too," the representative says. "My attitude is one of relief. Sure, I would have liked the order. Or rather, *my manager* would have. You'll think this is sour grapes, but it isn't. From the very beginning, I would have preferred not to have gotten the order at all. Now that I haven't, I'm glad."

"You are?" asks the customer, astonished. "Why?"

It is important to take the sales representative at his word. He isn't just letting himself down easily. Nor is he making a ploy. He means what he says. This conclusion comes as the result of a lot of study on his part, mostly about his customers' operations, where his products are used, and the effect his products have on those operations.

"What you needed from me—what you still need from me—isn't product. You can get product, good product, from several sources. I'm just one of them. But any one of three, four, or five of us can give you a high-performance product. One may perform a little bit better here, another there, but you can almost close your eyes and pick one and you'll never be embarrassed. So, since the product doesn't make much difference, I have decided I'd rather not compete on that basis. I want to do something else."

"Like what? Product is what selling is all about, isn't it?" the customer asks.

"We tend to make it seem that way," the representative says, "but it really isn't. In this case, as in so many others I study, product plays a minority role in producing the effect you want in your operations. Sure, it's got to work, and it's got to work well. But from that point on, the crucial difference comes from something else in almost every instance."

"Do you want to tell me what you think that is?"

"Sure," says the representative. "It's the part of the sale I specifically want to do: the application part, putting the product to work inside your operations to give you the results you need."

"We're pretty sure the product we're going to be receiving from your competitor will give us improved performance, better than we could get otherwise."

"That's not the type of performance I mean," the representative says. "I mean applying the product to your operations in such a way that more than your performance is improved. I want your profits to be improved, too. I want your costs to be reduced and the reduction dropped to your bottom line. I want there to be a positive effect on your sales as a result of an improved process. And I want the increased revenues from those added sales to go to your bottom line, too, in the form of added earnings. I don't just want to sell product or even install product to get a performance result. I want to turn performance improvement into profit improvement for you. If you don't get new profits, where's the payoff?"

What is the sales representative really telling his customer? He is saying that product alone rarely gives a customer what he needs: improved profits from the product's application. He is saying that performance improvement may not give the customer improved profits either, that it is possible to add significant value to a customer operation without the operation adding a commensurate value to profits. Not only is it possible, it is all too probable.

"But how could you do that with us unless you sold us the product?" the customer asks. "That's what you get paid for; that's what we buy. The application, the implementation, and all that, you just throw into the deal to make us satisfied, right?"

"Unfortunately, all too often that is true, and that's what is wrong here. You buy the less important part of what I sell. The more important part by far, knowledge of how to make the product generate new profits, you accept as the lesser half of the deal. You think its price is in the product, or that it's free. What you should do is just the opposite."

"How would that work?" the customer asks.

"First, you should decide among yourselves how much profit improvement you want or need in one of your operations that I can affect. Then you should call in me and my competitors and ask each of us how close we can come to meeting your objective. We'll go study your operations to determine our answer. When we come back to you, we will present you with an analysis of the improvement we can make in the dollars that particular process contributes to profit, the product system we would install to make it happen, and how much you'd have to invest with us to get the dollars back."

"And your competitors will give us the same kind of analysis," asks the customer, "so we can select the one with the highest profit improvement—not necessarily the highest performance capabilities or the lowest price?"

"Exactly."

"But under those conditions, what happens to the product?" asks the customer. "Would you feel differently about selling it to me then?"

"No. I still wouldn't sell it to you. Oh, I'd see that it got delivered on time, zero defects and all. I'd see that it got applied. But what I would be selling you is profits that its application could produce."

"You would still deliver and apply the product, wouldn't you?" the customer wants to know one more time.

"By all means," the representative assures him.

After a slight pause, the customer asks, "How soon can we expect your first shipment? I know of a competitor who almost thought he'd beaten you out."

The Best Business to Be in When You Sell Is a Business That Gets into the Customer's Business

Selling product brings every business eventually to the same point: its margins get beaten down. A business like that is not much fun and not very rewarding. The best time to go out of such a business may be sooner rather than later.

Sales manager: You've been a good customer for a long time now, so I thought I'd let you know first. At the close of the current quarter, we're going out of business.

Customer: Going out of business? I didn't even know you were in trouble.

Manager: We're not. At least, not yet. That's why we decided to go out of business now while we're still healthy and have money in the bank.

Customer: But if things are good, why close up?

Manager: We're not closing up, just going out of the business we've been in for half a century. We can see the handwriting on the wall: margins are shrinking, sales costs are rising. Every time we come up with a new product we get knocked off faster by competition.

Customer: What kind of business are you going to switch to?

Manager: We're going out of the business of manufacturing and selling products. We won't be a hardware company anymore.

Customer: We'll have a hard time replacing you as our preferred vendor. You've been built into a lot of our specs, you know.

Manager: You won't have to replace us. We'll still be able to supply you with our equipment. It's just that we won't be in the equipment business.

Customer: What will you be selling?

Manager: We won't really be selling, either. If you continue to do business with us, you'll be working with one of our consultants. We're moving to a service business.

Customer: What's the nature of the service?

Manager: Simply put, it's this: We're going to counsel you on how you can improve the profit contribution from the functions in your business where we have traditionally made our impact. We'll help you lower your costs in these functions. We'll even help you improve the quality of your end products and accelerate their output so you can increase your sales.

Customer: But haven't you always done that? I mean, isn't that the bottom-line reason why we've bought our equipment from you all these years and given your salespeople such open access to our business?

Manager: Exactly. You knew that. But we didn't. You knew you were buying maximum profit contribution, but that's not what we were selling. We sold you hardware. Even worse, we based our price on the cost of the hardware and on competitive pricing pressures. No wonder selling costs were so high: going over our product with you feature by feature, running performance tests, and all that. And no wonder our price was so low.

Customer: How will becoming consultants in profit improvement help you improve your own?

Manager: When you deal with us from now on, we'll come in and study the precise contribution to your costs that the functions we're expert in are making. Then we'll go back and design a system to reduce those costs, perhaps even eliminate them entirely. Finally we'll sit down with you and point out the new profits we can contribute to you and what return that represents on your investment with us. Our price will be based on your return, not on the hardware in the system.

Customer: What will the rest of the system contain?

Manager: Perhaps other pieces of equipment. Also services, many of which we've given away free just to sweeten our hardware for you. A training program for your people to help them get you on line with our equipment faster and with fewer problems. Maybe a lease-vs.-buy option.

Customer: And who's going to put this system together for us?

Obviously, every one will be custom-made for each individual situation.

Manager: Absolutely correct. Our consultant will be your maestro. He will manage the entire transaction.

Customer: Manage? Is that the word you're using instead of *sell?*

Manager: It's a far more accurate description of our sales force's new role. It's not to sell you our products. Instead, it's to manage the system so that it produces the end result of new profits for you.

Customer: Let me get this straight. Your salesperson won't be selling. He'll be managing—a kind of management consultant, right? And the product we buy from you won't be hardware. It will be improved profit. How's that?

Manager: Perfect. Can you see yourself doing business with us that way?

Customer: It will take getting used to, and there's one unsolved problem. Let's get back to price. If you base your price to us on the new profit you help us achieve, your prices will be higher than they are now, right? How can that help us improve our profit?

Manager: We'll be able to show you how your profit will be improved over and above any increase in what you pay us. As a matter of fact, that's our basic strategy. We'll always return you more dollars than you lay out. That's why you'll want to do business with us. We'll be a better deal for you than many other places you can put your money.

Customer: But I'm still going to want to ask you to lower your price.

Manager: Think of it this way. I have our first profit proposal here in my pocket to go over with you. It shows how we can go into your manufacturing function and squeeze out a little over $500,000 in costs. We can drop that money directly to your bottom line. Now tell me the price you'd be willing to pay to add half a million dollars to your profits this year.

Customer: If you're telling me that I shouldn't quibble over your charging me $50,000 or $75,000, I get the point. On a comparative basis, we're getting a good deal either way. But, of course, I'd still like to pay less.

Manager: You used to say the same thing when you bought hardware from us. We were never the low-priced supplier. Yet you did the major part of your business with us. Why?

Customer: You had the quality. We felt more comfortable with you. And it helped us in the long run to keep our costs down and stay operational. The same reasoning prevails for your new business, is that it?

Manager: Are there any questions you'd like to ask before I get into our first consultative proposal for you?

Customer: Just one. I wonder if our company could go out of our business, too, and do what you're doing. After all, we'd like to make more profit too.

Manager: Just do business with us. We'll save you the trouble. Here's your first $500,000 installment now.

Before You Plan Your Next Sale, Learn the Recipe for Selling à la Mode

There is really no such thing as "the customer's business" without understanding where it stands in its life cycle. Depending on whether it's growing or mature, you will have to deal with it in different ways.

Field sales manager: Before we start out on our call schedule together, why don't you brief me on the accounts we're going to see? That way I can get a quick preview of how you think about developing our business with them. Who's on first?

Sales Representative: A three-division conglomerate. It's a key account.

Manager: Do we sell to all three divisions?

Representative: No, just two. One's on the skids. Management is looking to sell it off, so I don't spend any time with that division.

Manager: Sounds like you're practicing business-mode analysis on your accounts. Are you?

Representative: If I am, I'm doing it without knowing what it's about. What's mode analysis?

Manager: It's the next step up from analyzing customers according to their potential purchases from us, the kind of classification that identifies our key accounts. Mode analysis enables you to identify how you should sell to your key accounts and what to push. You've just defined one of the modes.

Representative: Which one, the division on the skids? I'd call that a mode of *decline*.

Manager: And you'd be right. According to your way of looking at a declining business, you elect not to sell to it at all. Why is that?

Representative: I figure that its managers are not about to

30

spend a lot of money on a business they're trying to get rid of. Maybe just enough to keep it alive, but that's about all.

Manager: You equate that with no opportunity?

Representative: Not prime opportunity, that's for sure. Oh, I could probably sell some things to them. But they watch every penny they have. It would be tough.

Manager: On what basis could you sell to them?

Representative: Help keep them alive, keep them in business longer, stretch out their curve.

Manager: Why wouldn't they pay you to do that?

Representative: They probably would. But I'd have to prove to them that they could afford it. I'd have to sell on the lowest price possible.

Manager: Not necessarily. Suppose you sold on the highest value possible. Suppose you showed them how a reasonably small investment could help them create some cash flow internally and rescue dollars in the form of savings that they're now losing through unnecessarily costly or unproductive operations. Suppose the amount they saved was greater than the amount they had to spend with you. Could you make a deal?

Representative: It's problematic. Are you suggesting I try?

Manager: Only if you can cut their costs significantly and release those dollars for them to spend. It's worth thinking through. But mostly I agree with you. A customer in a declining mode is rarely a prime prospect. How about the other two divisions?

Representative: One is the company's basic business. Over half a century old, one of the big three in the industry. It has about a 25% share and fights hard every day to keep it.

Manager: What mode would you say it was in?

Representative: Established. Stodgy. Conservative. Which one do you like?

Manager: How about calling it *stable?* Loses a little here, gains a little there, but basically remains in the same position in its industry year after year. A reliable cash producer for the rest of the company.

Representative: That describes it to a T. I was hoping you wouldn't come down on it too hard, because it's a good customer of mine. The people there aren't always easy to do business with, but they try to be fair and there's no problem with their credit.

Manager: What problems do you have, though?

Representative: Price is the biggest. They bargain with me over pennies. They admit we have extra value in our performance, and they like our service. But they're the meanest price negotiators I've ever sold to.

Manager: Why do you suppose that is?

Representative: I'll have to guess: money must be important to them, even pennies. That suggests that they have the same problem selling their own products that we have in selling to them: a lot of pressure on margins. Why wouldn't they? That's what comes from being mature.

Manager: Something else comes from being mature, too. Any idea?

Representative: I'd say fear. When you're established and fighting to stay in place, you become fearful of anything that might upset the applecart, so you have to watch how you spend your money.

Manager: How do you sell to customers who are fearful of becoming unstable?

Representative: Ver-r-r-ry carefully. And with a lot of reassurance and comfort.

Manager: Are you doing that?

Representative: Probably not often enough. I get impatient. They take so long to make decisions: Everything goes out to bid, there must be three suppliers, and committees have to bless every expenditure request.

Manager: Now that you know why that's necessary for them, what can you do about it?

Representative: A couple of things occur to me. First, I can allow for it. I can say to myself at the outset, O.K., I'm in for a long haul on any major proposal. And I can be prepared to give them aid and comfort along the way.

Manager: One tried and tested form of comfort is to provide plenty of supportive evidence to back up your claims. Document everything. What's another?

Representative: Besides giving them evidence? Show them why it's safe to go ahead by promising them lower costs. Calculate the savings for them. There's nothing more comforting than the smell of money that you're going to save in your own operations.

Manager: Cost reduction is very important to a stable business. Very often, it provides funds that the customer is unable to get in any other way. And it offers a relatively safe way to get them. He doesn't have to go out into the dangerous world of the marketplace and gamble. But what about sales—can you help a stable customer there, too?

Representative: I think we have to. Reducing his costs is good; as a matter of fact, it's necessary. But the big opportunity to help him is through opening up sales avenues for him.

Manager: How are you doing that?

Representative: Showing him how our products can add performance value to his products and give him a higher price advantage, or a better market position, or a new approach to markets he hasn't been able to penetrate. When I'm able to do that, by the way, I can also get a higher price for our own products since I can sell them on the value they add to his.

Manager: This double-pronged approach to selling stable companies should keep you pretty busy. Does it take most of your time on the whole conglomerate account?

Representative: Most, but not all. I think it would be a tender trap for me if I allowed myself to devote too much time to its stable business. No matter how hard I justify price, the very real limits of the division's own profit position and the slow changes in its business put a ceiling on my opportunities. The business is aging slowly. I have to be careful not to be seen as aging with it.

Manager: How do you avoid it?

Representative: By making myself very visible and very helpful to the growth division. It's the conglomerate's newest business and the one chance the company has to break out of the commodity classification as an overall corporation.

Manager: That the third mode: *growth*. How do you zero in on its managers?

Representative: For a while, I carried over my habits in selling to them from my experience with the stable division. So I sold—or tried to sell—cost reduction, cost justification benefits. But there were no takers.

Manager: Why not?

Representative: All they care about is sales, sales, and more sales. They as much as told me to get lost unless I could contribute to their sales. When I reminded them that they were accumulating a lot of unnecessary costs in their drive for sales, they just smiled at me.

Manager: What did that teach you?

Representative: When you sell to a growing business, sell to aid its growth. By doing that, I give our own business the positioning of a growth company too, not just with them but internally, in our own management, too. My sales to this growth division have got to be the most profitable I make in this company because there's no price resistance and very little delayed decision-making.

Manager: You've told me a lot about how you sell. How about *what* you sell?

Representative: Sure, that's affected too. I have certain products that go into the growth division because they have a direct impact on stimulating its sales. To a lesser extent, I sell some of the same things to the mature division. But mostly there I sell our products that bring down its costs. I'll take the same approach when I review the declining division.

Manager: Are there any other aspects of mode analysis you'd like to discuss?

Representative: Just one. From a personal standpoint, which mode do you think of yourself as being in?

Manager: Why, I'm a growth manager, of course.

Representative: Good. Kindly remember that when I ask for a raise at my next performance review.

What's Another Word for Industry Specialist? Try Expert

Given the choice, customers will prefer to deal with suppliers who know two things best: the customer's business and how to apply expertise to make it more profitable.

Field sales manager: All right, if you had to pinpoint just one thing, what would you say is the main reason for your improved performance this year over last?

1st sales rep: Assured product supply—no shortages or allocations.

2nd rep: A much more consistent pricing policy.

3rd rep: We dropped many of the dogs, both products and customers.

4th rep: Better knowledge of our key customer industries.

Manager: All right, let me ask you this. On a scale of 1 to 10, how much do you think you know about each of the industries you call on?

1st rep: In the case of one, I'd say a 6. The other two I'd give a 3 or 4.

Manager: How much more effective do you think you could be if your knowledge were at the 7 or 8 level in all three industries?

1st rep: No doubt about it, my efficiency would jump. By how much? Would you believe maybe a third to a half?

Manager: That's a huge increase. I'll take it even at the lower number. Do the rest of you agree?

All reps: Yes.

Manager: Then let's face the inevitable question: Since the best way to get industry knowledge is to shape our selling strategies on the basis of it, should we go the route of the industry specialist? By industry specialist, I mean that every one of you would become highly knowledgeable in one or two industries and then you would specialize—sell only to these industries.

3rd rep: Why should I specialize? I'm proud to consider myself a generalist. Specialist in my product line, sure. But able to sell professionally to a wide range of industries. Call me a smokestack chaser if you like, but it's interesting and exciting. I learn a little about a lot of different industries.

Manager: What I want you to consider is the advantage of just the opposite: learning a lot about a small number of industries.

3rd rep: All I see are disadvantages. If I become a narrow specialist, I lose out on a lot of input. I limit myself. One of the attractions of selling is its diversity. By specializing, I learn more and more about less and less. What happens to my value?

Manager: It depends on what you consider the basis of your value to be. Is it surface knowledge? Or knowledge in depth? Is it the ability to promote and deliver products to everybody who has a generic need—or is it an ability to seek out specific needs because you know an industry? Is it to prescribe the exact product mix to solve comprehensive problems—in other words, sell systems of our products instead of individual items? Is it to prove how your prescription helps improve customer profit? That's something you can do only if you have an industry's cost structure down pat.

2nd rep: So I learn to do all those things. Then what? I'm locked into one industry and can't ever get out.

Manager: I don't know that becoming expert in an industry locks you into it. It gives you credibility. It enables an industry to credit you as our spokesman to it. And with credibility comes greater mobility.

4th rep: All right. I've gotten the industry's acceptance. How do I ever get out?

Manager: You mean, if you want to? You may like being an expert and enjoy the rewards it brings to you and your customers. But let's say you want to move into another industry, say after two or three years. You come to me and tell me it's time for a change.

1st rep: But then I'm a comparative novice in a new industry.

Manager: By the same token, someone else becomes a comparative novice, taking on *your* old job.

1st rep: That makes both of us just about what everyone is right now—jack of all trades and master of none.

Manager: Then you'd rather remain an expert: an industry-wise need seeker, systems prescriber, cost reducer, and profit improver. Not to mention our industry spokesman.

3rd rep: Yes and no. I'd still like to have my cake and eat it, too.

Manager: How about this, then? Every one of you gets to specialize in one industry. You cross territorial lines when you have to. Call in backup technical and financial support when you need it on proposals or service. Appear at the industry's association meetings, maybe speak at them and write articles in business publications. That's your No. 1 assignment. Then, as a fallback, you study another industry.

4th rep: That's better. But suppose I feel hemmed in by both industries. Can I transfer?

Manager: It's unlikely you'd dislike two out of two. Anyway, the answer's yes. As a matter of fact, I think the best policy is to make transfers available on demand every third year or so, to everybody. If you want to stay with your industry, you stay. If you want to move, you move. Either way, no penalties. If you move, though, you must train a successor and solidly position the succession before you can leave.

1st rep: I think that's fair. And I can see how I would deserve to be called a specialist if I stayed with a few industries over a long run. That's gratifying. But suppose I specialize in four, five, or six industries over a ten-year career. What would I be able to call myself then?

Manager: Sales manager.

When You Set Out to Penetrate a Key Account, Always Travel by Coach

Coaching and counselling with your own people can only go so far. Beyond that, you have to begin looking for coaches in the customer's business to take you the rest of the way.

Field sales manager: Last time we talked, gaining entry into your key accounts was your main problem—getting in at the right levels. How has that been going for you?

Sales representative: It still isn't easy. But I'm concentrating on it a lot less lately. I've discovered there's an even more important problem.

Manager: What's that?

Representative: Getting in is important. But the problem I call *getting in with* is crucial.

Manager: Getting in with whom? You know what you have to look for: decision makers who buy and the influencers who steer them. What's so complicated about that?

Representative: It's not so much that it's complicated. It's incomplete. There's a third person that I've got to be able to identify who doesn't make purchase decisions and doesn't necessarily influence them either. Yet I've discovered that this type of person can help me the most.

Manager: How would you describe him?

Representative: The best I can do so far is to think of him as my coach.

Manager: I thought that was my role with you.

Representative: It is—internally. But when I penetrate a customer company, I need someone there who can help me call the plays in his own ballpark.

Manager: Just exactly what does that mean? He certainly doesn't have to teach you how to sell, does he?

Representative: Well, in a way he does. Not in terms of selling skills or product knowledge, of course. But in a very critical subject area: how to apply my skills and knowledge to make the right impact on the right people in the right way at the right time.

Manager: In a nutshell, what play to call?

Representative: Right. Given my position on the field, how much time is left on the clock, and how tough the opposition is on the part of the decision makers and influencers.

Manager: What makes him so smart?

Representative: He's inside. Maybe that's a good second name for him: the *insider*. He knows what I don't know on the outside. Let me put it this way. Most of the time, I know *who* the right people are to sell and the *why* for them to buy. The coach knows *how* to sell them and a lot about the *when* and *where*.

Manager: What kinds of things is he likely to do for you?

Representative: He'll tell me where people's hot buttons are. He'll let me know if there's a budget available to buy what I'm selling. He'll tell me what issues to avoid, who the man with the monkey wrench is and how to keep out of his range. He'll advise me on how hard I need to push—should I low-key it or sell hard, expect a quick decision or let them know I'm prepared to do more homework.

Manager: He sounds invaluable. What sort of person is a coach likely to be?

Representative: It's easier to say what he *isn't* likely to be more than what he is. He's not a decision maker. He's not usually an influencer, either, although he may sometimes play the role of coach with influencers or decision makers. When he plays both roles—a coach to me and a coach to them—he's really invaluable.

Manager: When I asked you what sort of person he is, I meant things like this: what position, what longevity with the company, what career objectives of his own is he trying to achieve?

Representative: Let's take them one at a time. He can hold any one of several positions. That's what makes him hard to identify. One coach I had used to be sales manager and then moved to key account manager. I found another coach in the strategic planning function. He knew everybody in the company and everything the company was going to do. A third coach was an enlightened R&D

director (director emeritus, really). He knew everybody, especially the people who were most likely to do something.

Manager: So a coach can be anywhere, really. But a recurring characteristic in what you've said is that he must be somewhere that gives him broad exposure to the business and the key people in it.

Representative: That's true. And it leads us into the second characteristic of longevity. Coaches are long-timers. It takes quite a while for them to know the business and its people. That doesn't mean they're ancient, though some are. Ten years or so with the company might be a fair advantage. And that fact leads us into the third characteristic you asked about.

Manager: Career objectives?

Representative: Yes. That's as fuzzy an area as trying to pin down their titles. In one sense, I'm tempted to say they have no discernible career objectives—at least, they're nowhere near as obvious as the objectives of decision makers. Maybe what I should say is that coaches seem to have less selfish objectives or ones that are better integrated with those of the company as a whole. They help people like me because it helps them help their company.

Manager: They get their brownie points that way?

Representative: Some do. Others apparently aren't driven by the need to score points. They already have status or, even if they needed it once, they don't need it anymore. Sometimes their helpful role gives them all the points they need. After all, they're everybody's friend and nobody's competitor. That may be the best credential of all.

Manager: If we draw up a composite from what you've said, a coach would look like this: situated where he can view the company and its people from a function that lends itself to across-the-board access to the business (like sales, R&D, or planning); been there a relatively long time; and strongly identifies his own career objectives with those of the company at large. With that kind of profile, do you think you can identify him more easily now?

Representative: It will help, I suppose. But I'd still like to find a surer way, like walking into an organization and saying, "Take me to your coach!"

Manager: You can certainly say that implicitly by the way you act, can't you? You can make yourself highly visible as being interested in your customer, wanting to help him, having solutions to his problems, and offering yourself as a partner for customer people who want to solve those same problems. If you do these things, you'll be playing to a fourth characteristic of coaches you haven't mentioned yet.

Representative: What's that?

Manager: They're always looking for people to coach. By your trying to smoke them out, they will be able to smoke you out as being coachable.

Representative: Oh, I already knew that one.

Manager: Then how come you didn't say it?

Representative: I thought you'd be able to tell by the way I smoked you out—coach.

It's All Over for the Smiths and Joneses—Webbers Are the Only Ones Worth Hiring

Networking is a popular strategy for getting new jobs and advancing in existing ones. It can also be the strategy of choice for getting new sales and maintaining existing key accounts.

Field sales manager (to sales representative applying for a job): Before you start accusing me of discrimination, let me tell you that you're right. The only people I hire any more are webbers.

Representative: So if my name isn't Webber, that lets me out, right?

Manager: It's not your name. It's your sales strategy. When I say I want webbers, I mean spinners of customer relationships, network builders, people who weave connecting links between themselves and customer decision makers and purchasing influencers.

Representative: If that's what you mean by a webber, then I qualify.

Manager: Let's see whether you do. What's a webber's web composed of?

Representative: Well, the only way I know to connect myself to a customer decision maker is with benefits. They're the only reason anyone does business with me.

Manager: What kind of benefits?

Representative: That depends on who the decision maker is. If he is at an operating level, say, in marketing or product development, I'll try to weave a web around him based on the performance benefits of my product: how it can help him improve the working of his own products so he can improve his sales and profits. On the other hand, if he is at a purchasing or financial level, I'll web us

42

together on the basis of value-to-price ratio. That means I'll justify price by emphasizing the value of the benefits that the price pays for. I'll quantify reduced costs or show how he can get a higher price for the new benefits.

Manager: Suppose the decision maker is at the top management level?

Representative: When I'm lucky enough to get up there, I'll sell value, too. But I'll connect it with my effect on his profits. I call it the "contribution benefit."

Manager: All right, you seem to have the spirit. But to be a real webber, you have to apply your spirit in customer relationships. To me, at least, that means a webber is really five people rolled up into one. First of all, he is a *grower*. He believes that every network of customer relationships has the capacity for growth. He never stops pushing for that growth. When his customers see him coming, they say, "Here comes the person who keeps wanting our business together to grow." Can you think of a second webber characteristic?

Representative: In addition to being a grower, he'd better be an *initiative taker*. Webs wear thin. Decision makers change jobs, get promoted or transferred, get spun into one of our competitor's webs. You have to take the initiative all the time to strengthen your network.

Manager: How do you do that?

Representative: You make sure you're a *mover*. Every network of benefits is like a highway for movement. That really is my "territory." I try to keep moving up and down my territory all the time, gaining access to my decision makers by delivering benefits to them. Keeping in motion in this way is more important to me than the details of how I move. Moving is even more important than having a specific solution available before you begin to move.

Manager: So you're a mover. But what do you do when you can't move, when you run into resistance?

Representative: Every web is a mixture of readiness to accept my benefits and resistance to them. That's why I try to be a *leaner*. I'm always putting pressure on my webs. Where they give, I move. Where I feel blocked, I stop moving and just lean. Sometimes the roadblock gives when I lean on it. When it doesn't, rather than have my movement stopped, I'll lean somewhere else and find a readiness

I can exploit. Most of the time, it's better to expend my energy this way than to try to overcome resistance.

Manager: Do you go back periodically to lean on the resistance and see if it's ready to give?

Representative: Yes, partly out of curiosity, partly out of pride. But I've learned at least one thing about webs: you can't just lean on them; sometimes you have to be a *tugger.* You don't tug only in one area of resistance, either. If you do, the web simply springs back into place when you let go. I tug in several places at once. That way, the web changes its shape temporarily and may open up new roadways for me.

Manager: What kind of reaction do you get from customers as a result of your being a grower, an initiative taker, a mover, a leaner, and a tugger?

Representative: If I do all those things professionally—and, after all, that's my job—they see me as their partner in weaving webs that *they* depend on. They need to tie into good, dependable sources—not just product supply, but sources of information, advice, and common interest that help them improve their profits. That's why an ideal customer is a webber, too. He's always moving, leaning, and tugging. When both of us are doing our jobs properly, we build strong, active webs that support a lot of traffic.

Manager: You certainly talk a good web. I'd like to see one of your webs firsthand and get a look at one of your partners.

Representative: In that case, just look in the mirror.

What's Selling? It's Taking Customers Who Look Good and Making Them Look Better

Instead of complaining how customer purchasers make you look bad, there's money to be made by asking how you can make them look good.

Field sales manager: What do you think about your relationship with the purchasing agent—is he your adversary or your partner?

Sales representative: Half and half. He's my adversary when he tries to cut me down on price. He's my partner when he gets in trouble or when he wants to take credit for my ideas.

Manager: With partners like that, who needs adversaries? But seriously, if you could do what you wanted to do with him, what would your objective be?

Representative: To make his job easier. To help him improve his contribution and make him look good.

Manager: Why would that be your No. 1 objective?

Representative: Selfish reasons, for one thing. If he looks good, I look good. But there's another reason, too. He doesn't have many opportunities to look good to his own management. He's usually at the tail end of the power chain, and nobody looks good down there.

Manager: How can you help him?

Representative: First of all, by understanding how his managers perceive him. They see him primarily in one way: as their cost-reduction agent. That's their lifetime conception of him. If he does the job badly, he goes. If he does it well, he stays. But there's no place for him to go anywhere else in management. He's stuck for life.

Manager: Not all purchasing agents you deal with are in dead-end jobs, are they?

Representative: Maybe "all" is too strong. But certainly most of them are. Where are they going to go, based on what they know about managing a business or about their business as a whole? You could fit both into a thimble.

Manager: So what can you do about that?

Representative: That's the second part of my answer. I can probably help the purchasing agent more than he can help himself. Suppose he wants more management exposure. Well, so do I, and with the same people in his organization. By working with him, I can help him get upstairs and command management attention.

Manager: Why can't he do that for himself?

Representative: He lacks management credibility for anything but cost control. Management dictates policy and he's expected to execute it. He's in a reactive role. It's difficult for him to take the initiative.

Manager: How do you help him do that?

Representative: By fertilizing him with better ways to do his job: recommendations for controlling costs that he can't think up for himself or that he can't implement without my help.

Manager: How is that going to help us sell?

Representative: Every recommendation I make to him about reducing costs will be based on one or more of our products. He'll have to buy from me in order to get the benefit.

Manager: And when he does, he'll be able to present himself to his upstairs management as the greatest little idea man in the company. They won't even know you're alive!

Representative: That's all right at first. That's how he'll begin to look good in his own organization. His bosses won't know where his new ideas come from, but he will. I figure he'll be back for more.

Manager: When do you get into the act?

Representative: Oh, there'll come a time when I'll sell him on an application that's a bit more complex than the ones that have gone before. I'll make it clear that a little help from me might make the difference between success and failure for his proposal. By then, either he'll have enough confidence to invite me to come along with him, or I'll just have to work on him some more.

Manager: What about our competitors while all this is going on? Won't they be trying to make your friend the purchasing agent look good, too?

Representative: Sure they will. But my job is to make him look better than anyone else can. Otherwise, who needs me? Not him. Not you. Besides, I have an ace up my sleeve.

Manager: You mean, another way to make him look good besides better cost control?

Representative: Exactly. As I see his job, it has two sides. One is cost reduction. By keeping my price low, he takes care of that. But by showing him how his cost burden is kept low even when he pays my higher price, I'm helping both of us achieve our objectives. So much for costs. Are you ready for my ace? I'm also going to help him make a contribution to increased sales.

Manager: He's already supposed to be doing that by purchasing only according to specifications, making sure we're a quality house and all that. What more can he do?

Representative: Once I get him to look good in the cost arena, I'm going to tell him about some of the buying preferences I know his company's customers have. No, I'm not going to make a salesperson out of him, or a market researcher. I'm just going to round off his education. When he goes upstairs with new ideas, I want him to be able to recommend us because we can best help meet his company's *customers'* needs.

Manager: Give me an example.

Representative: Well, I get around and he doesn't, so I'm in a good position to keep him informed about market needs. I can say to him, "One of your products should have this or do that—or stop doing that. Here's the evidence. If we can add the new benefit or correct the existing problem, we can open up new sales opportunities. Here's my recommendation."

Manager: And if it works and they sell more, we sell more to them, right?

Representative: Right. And then maybe for the first time, the purchasing agent's management sees him as a contributor to new sales dollars. Instead of just looking good, he looks better.

Manager: You've done something he couldn't do for himself. But why do you think that being a contributor to new sales dollars is so important to a buyer?

Representative: Because that's the reason everybody in business gets up in the morning: to sell something.

Manager: The morning's almost half over now. You'd better get going.

2

Top-Level Selling

Getting Upstairs, Where Decisions Are Based on Value

Instead of Going Around the Purchaser, Why Not Try Going Around with Him?

When you want to sell upstairs, purchasers can be partners or roadblocks. A lot depends on which of the two you yourself are.

Field sales manager (beginning a counselling session): What would you say are the main stumbling blocks to improving your performance?

Sales representative: That's easy: purchasing agents.

Manager: But they're our customers. How can they be your obstacles?

Representative: They're always taking me down on price. They don't give me the information I need to plan ahead for their companies' needs. They keep me from having access to other decision makers in their companies. That's three; how's that for starters?

Manager: Not bad. What can I do to help?

Representative: Tell me how I can get around the purchasing agent so I can be a salesman, not just a price cutter or a glorified order filler.

Manager: Suppose you got around him—what then? Where would you make your call?

Representative: Wherever I wanted to. I'd see product management, engineers, R&D people, division managers—even the president himself.

Manager: All right. Starting today, you have my permission to go right to the top of every customer account you have. There's only one catch: First you have to tell me what you'll say when you get there.

Representative: That's easy. I'll say the same things I say to the PA. But I'll have a far more responsive ear.

Manager: On the contrary. I think you'll have total deafness. What you'll do is bring the president down to the level of his purchasing department, except that he won't have the PA's interest in things like our product specifications, terms, and other finite details. Any self-respecting president would take you—or throw you—right back down the stairs.

Representative: O.K., I'll tell him something else: why we're better than the competition.

Manager: He won't be able to tell from your say-so. He has people under him who determine that. You'd be back downstairs again.

Representative: Why our product's better made, more durable, more reliable.

Manager: That's why he has an engineering department. It's downstairs again.

Representative: Why we're safe and comfortable for him to do business with because we're ethical.

Manager: That's something for his legal department to worry about. It's downstairs, across the hall from engineering.

Representative: If you're going to say that about everything, then there's only one thing left to tell the president: why I can't work with his purchasing agent.

Manager: That's a problem for personnel. . . .

Representative: I know. Downstairs. So what do I say?

Manager: Until you know the answer to that question, you can't go. Let's see what you can do to improve what you're doing now. So far, I've got to be grateful that you *haven't* been able to get around the purchasing agent. The way I see it, he's been protecting you. What can you do for him?

Representative: Other than cut back even more on price, you mean? Well, I suppose I could see if he knows what's on the president's mind so I could learn what to talk about if I ever get upstairs.

Manager: That's an improvement. But what can you do for him?

Representative: Maybe work up something to talk to the president about that would get us both upstairs, give us both visibility and a chance to learn something about the company's needs.

Manager: Few purchasing agents get that sort of exposure. That may be why they don't tell sales representatives what the future needs of their companies will be. They may not know. Going upstairs together under the buddy system is one way to help both of you. What's another?

Representative: Give the PA some ammunition so he can go upstairs himself. It doesn't have to be to the president. But he should be able to go to any of his research or planning or operating people and tell them he has a solution to one of their problems. And I should be the source of that solution.

Manager: That sounds like an ideal relationship you're contemplating. Suppose you don't have such a cooperative PA. What if he doesn't *want* exposure to his upper-level management—and he doesn't want you to have it either?

Representative: Then I'll sit down with him and say, "I've got to make some new solutions known inside your company. My preference is to do it with you. If you'd rather not participate, no hard feelings. It would help your company and help me, too, if you would introduce me to the right people. But if you'd rather not do that either, I'll search them out on my own. In any event, our relationship—yours and mine—won't be adversely affected in any way."

Manager: If your searching out gets you all the way upstairs to the president, what will you say to him?

Representative: Why, I'll just tell him what a great purchasing agent he has.

It's So Hard to Get a Shot at the Top Man—Don't Get Shot Down When You Do

"I finally did it," the sales representative says. "I got upstairs today—I saw the president himself. It took me over a year but today I did it."

"Congratulations," the manager says. "What did you say to him?"

"I told him why his company ought to be a customer of ours: that we have the best product, the best service, the best terms."

"I hope you resisted the temptation to tell him what fools his people are for not buying from us. After all, he may have hired some of them himself," the manager says.

"Don't worry, I was polite. But I did make sure he knew one thing: We're the quality supplier. I put him on our mailing list so he'll be able to keep in touch."

"So how many dollars' worth of business did he sign off on?" the manager asks.

"Nothing yet. But I left him thinking."

Every year, after they have finally made a sales call at the top, sales representatives leave customer presidents thinking. But what are the presidents thinking about? "Why did I ever let that salesman in here anyway? How can anyone spend 30 minutes talking about *his* company, *his* product, *his* services and never once relate any of it to *my* business? What makes a salesman think that as president I'm interested in how products perform or what they cost? Doesn't he have any idea at all about what my job is like?"

The answer, unfortunately, is generally no. Sales representatives, and just as often their managers, devote untold energy to planning and scheming so that they can stand before customer presidents and sell to them. Many actually make it to the top. Few sell when they get there. Their high failure rate is not due to lack of knowledge of *their* business. The fault is that they know little or nothing about the president's business.

Presidents are operating people. They are pragmatists because they are judged pragmatically by the people who evaluate them: directors, shareholders, the investment community, competitors, and their employees. For this reason, they are results-oriented. The results to which they orient themselves, however, are not the performance results of how suppliers' products work. A president's results are financial. They appear not so much on the top line, where his costs are, but on the bottom line that shows his profits.

Although presidents may listen, they rarely hear anything that does not have an important implication for their profits. When their own people talk to them, this is the *only* context in which a proposal stands a chance. Outside suppliers must address a president the same way. Otherwise they will be talking to themselves and wasting a rare opportunity.

Presidents get up in the morning and go to bed at night with one overriding issue on their minds: How can I improve our profits? They look for help, most of the time in vain. When their own people come in, they are usually asking for money. They talk about how little cost they will add to the budget. They may promise payback or profit, but it may be indefinite or prolonged or chancy. Then, in the midst of all these demands, a sales representative appears. What does he offer? The chance to add even further to costs.

"If you had to make your call all over again," the manager says, "what would you do differently?"

"First of all, I would burn some midnight oil studying the customer's business so I knew more about where our product lines best fit. I would look for a specific problem area the customer has that we can solve. Then I'd work with our financial people to calculate how much money the customer can add to his operations by doing business with us."

"How much would you talk about our products?" the manager asks.

"Hardly any. He's not a product specialist."

"How much would you tell him about our competitors?"

"Nothing, probably. He's more concerned about competitors of his own."

"What about price?" the manager persists.

"I'd turn it around. I'd talk instead about what he would get for his money, not how much he had to spend to get it. I'd talk results."

If presidents spoke their minds to their supplier sales representatives, they might well pose one question to every sales representative who crosses their threshold: What are you going to do to help me run my business better? The answer they are looking for will not be found among the typical responses—sell you something, improve the quality of your operations, raise productivity and morale, or any of the other old standbys.

"If you could go back there right now," the manager says, "and say only one sentence, what would it be?"

"Something like, 'How would you like to have me improve your profits?' "

"Do you think he'd hear you?"

"I don't know yet. But I'm going to do my oil burning this weekend and then go back and find out. If he hears me half as well as I've heard you, I'll be all right."

A President Who Says "Let's Talk" Doesn't Want Your Words of Wisdom—He Wants Your Dollars of Profit

When the president, or any member of corporate top management, invites his sales and marketing people to enter into a dialogue with him, he gives them a golden opportunity to communicate their needs in a forum where something can be done about them. And he is serious. An alert management upholds its half of the dialogue by focussing the discussion on the requirement for more profitable sales, rather than merely sales volume or share of market. In this way, management is doing what it does best: setting objectives. Carrying them out is the province of the sales force.

Sales people often lose out, however, because they are unable to speak the language of management in requesting the tools they believe they need to achieve management's objectives. As a result, little or nothing gets accomplished. For example, at a sales meeting of a major diversified manufacturer, the president lays his message flat out to the entire department. "Concentrate on our key product lines," he says, "and within each line, concentrate on the key products, putting most of your efforts into selling to top customers. Now tell me," he asks, "what can we in corporate management do to help?"

Eventually, a sales manager raises his hand. "When are we going to resume our corporate advertising campaign?" he inquires. The president stares at him. Because the question was not asked in the language of management, the president is apparently translating it to himself. Finally, he asks, "Why?"

"Well," the man says, "it did a lot of good for us out in the trade." The president stares at him again. "How much good?"

"I have the feeling that it helped some of us a lot. I'm pretty sure it helped me. I can't prove it, of course, if that's what you mean."

By then, the president realizes the same thing, so he turns to the next question. It is unlikely that the president feels any sense of urgency about resuming the corporate advertising campaign.

It is an oversimplification to say that the sales executive and his president are not communicating. The president is speaking the language of management. The manager is not. If he were, he could have known what was coming and, preferably, been in a position to deal with it.

The language of management is different from the language of salesmanship. In many of its functions, it is *evaluative*, rather than action-oriented. It is designed to qualify the recommendations suggested to top management, which is under constant pressure from each element of the business to "do something." Management obviously cannot do everything. Consequently, it must evaluate by questioning. It asks questions of its own in response to questions put to it. The asker must have all the answers, not management. Only if all the answers are forthcoming will management stop asking questions and take action. Therefore, the sales manager's question about corporate advertising might better have been phrased in management's language, something like this:

"Last year my average cost per sale was $39. The year before, it was $43. This year, so far, it seems to be working its way up to $43 again. In checking with the six other regional managers, I discovered that four of them have observed the same changes in their cost structure. The major variable we had going for us last year but not this year or two years ago was corporate advertising.

"Furthermore, the annual reports of our two major competitors also show a correlation between higher dollar sales and the years in which they ran corporate advertising. There are, of course, other variables that could account for these results—an industrywide price decrease last year, a strike in our own plants two years ago, and two new product introductions this year.

"I'd like to suggest we consider a six-month test of a $25,000 corporate advertising campaign directed to key accounts. This should encompass our capability story with regard to our key products, and should influence enough sales to pay for the campaign 50 times over, at least."

A reply along these lines shows that the marketer has anticipated management's questions and that he can express his answers to them in terms that management understands. Since all top managers generally ask the same basic questions, every sales executive can prepare himself in advance and thus help to improve communications between the field and corporate headquarters. Here are four of the most frequently asked questions and a brief statement of their purpose.

1. Why? This management question seeks to learn the objective of a recommendation. Does it promise to add value in terms of profit? Because of this, every suggestion from managers should be positioned directly or indirectly as a cause of incremental profit. Corporate advertising that does "a lot of good out in the trade" may not be adding a penny's worth of profitable sales. In fact, it may be adding only to the cost of sales. When the president asks why, he wants a response in terms of new profits: a lot of dollars, rather than "a lot of good."

2. How much? The object of this question is to learn the cost-effectiveness of a recommendation. What will it accomplish over and above its cost? Every suggestion should therefore prove its promise of adding profit by giving management a number. Corporate advertising that "helped some of us a lot" is unquantified. It cannot be measured. And if it cannot be measured, it will probably not be acted on. The inability to prove the "how-muchness" of a proposal, or at least to document it by experience, is almost always self-defeating.

3. What else? When top management asks this question it is trying to find out what other options have been considered and why they have been rejected. Are there any other things that could be done for the same amount of money, or even less, that would bring better results? Every suggestion should therefore tell management what to compare against its promise of profit. Corporate advertising may or may not be the best alternative to boost sales. But management will never know unless other sales adjuncts are comparatively evaluated and shown to be less cost-effective. The comment "I can't prove it" shows that no such comparisons have been made.

4. What next? This question seeks to anticipate the consequences of accepting a recommendation and to determine how much money is required to capitalize it. In short, what is the company letting itself in for, how fast can it pull out, and how can it squeeze every bit of mileage out of the investment? Thus, suggestions from the field should tell management how to integrate each proposal fully with current company strategy and how to "disintegrate" it in case it doesn't pay off. Such safeguards assure management that it will be able to amortize an investment to the fullest or, in the event of failure, cut the loss before it reaches disastrous proportions.

Ideally, management should have no questions left to ask when a presentation from the field is put in proper "managementese." And, as every salesman knows, when the prospect runs out of questions, it's time to ask for the order.

When You've Got Fifteen Minutes to Sell to the Man at the Top, the Most Important Thing to Remember Is Not to Sell

"You're the third vendor from your industry that I've seen this past month," the customer's department manager says. "The other two got in here by subterfuge. They said they weren't selling anything but had vital information for me. It turned out the information was about their new product line, so I sent them back downstairs to purchasing. You'll make the same trip if that's why you're here."

"I already wrote you why I wanted 15 minutes with you," the representative says.

"Yes, I have it right here." The customer holds up the letter. "In 15 minutes you're going to help me improve my operation, the one I spend ten hours a day working on week in and week out. But please forgive my skepticism. What do you have in mind?"

The representative has achieved his first objective. He has gotten upstairs to see a management decision maker. His next few words will determine whether he is going to make it pay off, not just for himself but for his customer. It would be one thing to come away with an order. But it would be even better to make this the start of a partnership with the customer that could serve as the context for future orders. That is his second objective.

"I decided I wouldn't just go on selling to your company anymore," the representative says. "We don't happen to have a new product line right now, so you don't have to worry about my

61

springing one on you. In fact, we believe that our present products do the job for you just fine. That's why I wanted to see you. Even if we make our products better, we aren't going to help you improve your operations all that much, certainly not in areas where your performance could have a significant benefit. Your problems don't have very much to do with our products, or with our prices, either. Would you let me tell you where I think you could really use some help?"

"That's why you're here," the customer says, pointing to the letter. "You've got about ten minutes left."

"As I see it," the representative says, "your costs and productivity problems aren't with our products or those of our competitors. They all work and work well, so much so that there's little to choose among them. That is why we all have to bargain over price with your purchasing people, which is foolish. Instead, I'd like to help you attack two problems. One is the way your operation is organized; the other is the turnover in your workforce that reduces its level of productivity."

The representative stops and holds his breath. The customer sits there, staring at him. It is a tense moment. Any second, the representative expects the manager to say, "What makes you an expert in our operation? You're a vendor. Go back downstairs where you belong." But instead he asks, "What about the way my operation is organized; what about our productivity? What do you find wrong with them?"

"In general, two things," says the representative. "They're costing you more than they should, and they're reducing your output, which affects your sales. Let me give you just one example in each category. Every year I see dozens of operations like yours. Not just the one you manage but those of your competitors as well. Everyone does something better than the others, but nobody puts it all together. One major element is your layout. Just the way you have your work area organized can add or subtract thousands of dollars' worth of wasted time every year through the way work flows. I'd like to study your workflow from the vantage point of my experience and see if I can save those thousands of dollars for you. It might require some procedural changes, or maybe some structural changes in the workspace. Perhaps both. But the results will justify them and, in the long run, you could come out way ahead."

"O.K., so much for organization. Now give me your training course, the other area you mentioned," says the customer.

"If we change the way work flows, of course we'll have to change how we train the people who do it. But that's only one aspect. The major constraint to improved productivity in just about every operation I've observed is the way its people perform. Sure, it's important to give them the best products that your vendors can supply. But what good is that if your people aren't trained to use them in the best way? Right now, much of the value you've paid for in products is wasted because your employees can't put them to work properly. I think you should give your people adequate products and superior training rather than the other way around."

The customer stands up and goes to a file cabinet. "Here," he says. "This is a schematic drawing of our floor layout. All the workstations are numbered consecutively so you can see how the production flows. Take it and come back with your suggested revision in ten days. As for training, you probably have a program for our people somewhere up your sleeve. Come back to me with that in ten days, too. There's one thing I'll be looking for in both of your proposals: How much money will I save on the one hand, and how much new output will I get on the other? Oh yes, one more thing. My same rule still applies: Don't try to sell me any of your products or I'll send you back to purchasing."

The representative reaches into his briefcase. "While I'm doing the assignment you've just given me, I'd like to leave these case histories behind for you to read," he says. "They'll give you an idea of what to expect from me in ten days. Don't worry, there's no product sell in them. They're just accounts of companies that have done with us the same thing you've asked me to try to do for you."

"So you do this for a living?" the customer asks. "How do you make money this way? Do you sell operation analyses, or training programs, or what? Suppose I like something you come up with and I want to implement it; how do we do business?"

"I sell only one thing," the representative says, "and I've already promised you that it wasn't products. I sell improved profits, either through reduced costs or increased productivity and sales. Sometimes I can improve a customer's profits both ways. That's what I'm going to try to do for you. But all I really sell is profits. The layout of your operations, training programs for your people, products—these are all ways that I make profits happen for you. That's why I'm here talking to you. If I were just selling products, I'd be down in purchasing. You said so yourself."

"But the products come along as part of the way you improve our profits. Right?"

"Yes, but since I don't sell them, you don't have to buy them," the representative says.

"Funny thing," says the customer. "I have a feeling I already have."

When You Sell Upstairs, Take Along Your Topside Dictionary or You'll Be Talking to Yourself

When customer top managers talk, it's a good idea to listen. But when you get the chance to talk to them, will they return the compliment? Only if you speak the only language they know and love . . . and it isn't product or price.

Field sales manager: How long has this been going on—hearing footsteps when you're out making calls?

Sales representative: For the last several weeks. I'll sit down with a purchasing agent and somewhere along in the conversation I'll hear footsteps upstairs. Competition has preempted me and sold above me. Sometimes I think I can hear them walking over me right in the middle of my presentations.

Manager: How did they get up there?

Representative: That's what I'd like to know. When I ask my customers what's going on, they tell me about higher-level decision makers getting more and more into the act, about specifications being influenced by our competitors long before bids go out. All that's left for me is the crumbs.

Manager: Haven't you ever been upstairs yourself?

Representative: Sure, I've been there. But its been a quick trip up and back for me every time.

Manager: Why is that?

Representative: Well, when I get up there I just don't seem to be able to demand anyone's attention for very long. Oh, people at that level are very polite and they have a good deal of sensitivity. I guess that's how they get there in the first place. But they use their politeness to turn me away, not to buy from me.

Manager: What are you trying to sell them?

Representative: My regular stock in trade, what else? Our

company reputation, our product benefits, how we rate ourselves superior to competition. Oh, yes, and our prices, which I always remind customers are fair and equitable for both of us.

Manager: No wonder they turn you away. I'm surprised that they're so polite about it.

Representative: What do you mean? Wasn't it you yourself who told us at last year's conference to "tell our story, tell our story big, and tell it up and down the line"? Well, I've been telling it up the line and it hasn't worked.

Manager: Your memory's excellent. But only as far as it goes. I also said something like, "Be sure to tailor our story to the specific interests at each level." Don't you remember the "Level with Every Level" theme?

Representative: Sure, I've been doing that. The higher up the organization chart I go in a customer company, the less steak and the more sizzle I give them.

Manager: Maybe we need to redefine what you mean by *steak.*

Representative: As I told you: product benefits, price advantages, competitive terms, all the reasons why we're better.

Manager: That's probably the problem. The higher you penetrate a customer's business, the less interest anybody has in why *we're* better. Take that as an axiom. What they're interested in is how to make *themselves* better.

Representative: Isn't one of the ways by doing business with our company?

Manager: Only if you relate our advantages to theirs. And you can't do that by talking product and price—or even pride. What do you think their cares and concerns really are?

Representative: Well, many of the upper-level people I've called on have profit responsibility for their operations. Some of them even refer to their departments or divisions as profit centers. So I guess profit would be one of their major concerns.

Manager: Do you suppose that you could earn more than their polite interest if you talked to them about how doing business with us can help their profit?

Representative: Sure, and I do. I always talk about our competitive pricing policies. They know that means we can be a low-cost supplier and help their profit that way.

Manager: But every supplier can say the same thing to them.

And does. Besides, that's why upper-level decision makers have purchasing agents. They're the price dealers. What do you suppose top and middle managers want to hear about profit?

Representative: Something other than price. Something different from what every other supplier can tell them. Say, maybe that's why suppliers have such a hard time getting upstairs in the first place: The people up there have all heard the same story from all of us, so why should they listen to it again from me?

Manager: Exactly. They probably know it better than you do. After all, you only learned it from me. They learned it from dozens of people like us. But what *haven't* they learned enough about from anybody they deal with?

Representative: How to make more profit for their profit centers in ways other than low price and favorable terms from their suppliers.

Manager: All right, so why not take advantage of that need? Why not talk to them about making more profit and how we can help?

Representative: But not by talking about our product or price?

Manager: Not initially. That's not what they want to hear, remember? They need to learn. What do you have to tell them about their problems and opportunities that they haven't heard a hundred times before?

Representative: Well, certain aspects of their profit centers' operations are right down our alley. That's why they use our product. We probably know more about running these operations that they do. We know how to run them most economically, for instance; or how to get a better finished product out the door so they don't suffer recalls; or how to increase the speed of their materials handling; hey, we even know their warehousing.

Manager: Do you think they'd sit still if you talked to them about any one of these things and told them how we can help—with our products and services, of course?

Representative: Why not? They're thinking about those things all the time, anyway, aren't they? So I wouldn't be interrupting them. In fact, I'd be gearing right in with them. I could even introduce my calls by telling them I know what their most important problems are and that's why they should be interested in what I have to say.

Manager: It's what you say from that point on that will make you or break you. Are you sure you know how to speak in management language: from what I call the "Topside Dictionary of Selling"?

Representative: What are the key words?

Manager: Profit is the most important one. Relate what you're selling to the specific contribution it can make to customer profit. Quantify as much as you can. Profit isn't an idea to be talked about, you know. It's numbers that management takes to the bank.

Representative: Any other words?

Manager: The way you express profit can be crucial. Whenever possible, work profit out to its net contribution. That's usually about half of gross profit, allowing for taxes. So speak of it as *net profit after taxes*. Call it *incremental profit* to remind customers that it's over and above what they've already budgeted for. And that they wouldn't have a chance at it without doing business with you.

Representative: Any more?

Manager: Just one. *Return on investment,* or *ROI.* Make clear to topside customers that their spending with you represents an investment on which they will get a return. On the basis of your net profit figures, calculate the rate of their return. That's the way they look at their investments, you know: 3% back on this, 12% on that. Let them know where every major purchase from us will rank.

Representative: If I keep talking like that—profit, return on investment—they may forget that I'm a salesman who has a product to push. What then?

Manager: That's fine with me. If they forget about product, maybe they'll forget about pressuring us on price. And if they forget about price and think of doing business with us as an investment instead of a cost, there's no telling how high our own profit and return on investment will go.

3
Knowing the Customer

Being Able to Talk to the Customer About the Customer

If You're Overselling in Mature Markets, It's Likely You're Underknowing About New Opportunities

"You're overselling," the manager says.

"That's a new one," the sales representative answers. "At the last counselling session we had, you accused me of underselling. How did I go from one to the other?"

"You didn't," is his manager's answer. "You're still underselling. But the reason you're underselling is because you're overselling."

What sounds like double-talk is actually the kind of straight talk that will be heard with increasing frequency in many industries over the next few years. It is a sign of the changes that are taking place in sales strategy as the basic concepts of marketing penetrate more deeply into the selling functions. The concept underlying the conversation between the representative and his manager is the principle of market segmentation.

Any company that has been in business for a few years or more is governed by the 80-20 rule. Up to 80% of its profitable sales volume comes from as few as 20% of all its customers. These are the company's major markets. They may also be its most mature markets—markets where volume has topped out and where individual shares of market have become fixed. If this is the case, further concentration of sales pressure may no longer produce a cost-effective increase in profits on sales.

This does not always mean that sales themselves cannot be increased. They may be susceptible to boosting on a unit or dollar basis. But their profit contribution may be slight or nonexistent because their cost will exceed their value. The effectiveness of every cost dollar spent will be disproportionately small compared to what the same dollar might be able to earn elsewhere. Hence the key point: When major markets become mature, where should sales dollars be heavied up?

"How can you stop overselling?" the manager echoes his representative. "By selling more in undersold markets—markets where we can grow our business on a high margin per unit basis, not where more volume is profitless."

"But people in our present markets know us. We're a major factor," says the sales representative.

"Unfortunately, so are our competitors."

"We've beaten them before. We've eaten their lunch with some major pieces of business."

"Sure we have," the manager counters, "and the next thing we knew, they were eating our lunch with someone else. When the music stops, we've all spent a lot of money on promotion and given away a lot of product. All for what? Each of us is right back where we started from in our volume and our shares. Only our profits are down."

The combination of mature markets and mature, competitive supply choices spells low opportunity for a profit breakthrough. To go on emphasizing sales in this situation is to throw a resistible force at an immovable object. The solution lies elsewhere. It requires a strategic reallocation of sales resources, cutting them back in mature markets and increasing them in markets of faster growth.

"Let me make something perfectly clear," the manager continues. "I don't want you to undersell in our mature markets in an absolute sense. It's comparatively speaking that I want underselling—compared to what you've been doing. My real objective is to have you find out exactly the right level for your sales pressure in these markets where we're well established. Then I want you to maintain it so that we hold our own. The time you free up will go to new market invasion."

"Invasion?" the representative says. "You mean *evasion*. How can I invade a market I don't know anything about and that knows little or nothing about me? My temptation is to find every way in the book to avoid it."

"You have an alternative, you know. You can wait until our competitors learn how to meet its needs and sew up the best accounts for themselves. Then we'll know everything we have to know about another mature market."

The need to know about a new market before trying to sell into it is the prerequisite to avoid overselling in well-established markets. Homework is the key to sales success. As a rule, the length of the sales cycle once penetration of a new market has begun is directly proportional to the amount and accuracy of market analysis carried out beforehand.

The core question is still, Who is the decision maker, and what are his needs? But in today's more refined sales environment, that must be supplemented by other questions. How much is the customer's problem costing him? By how much can we reduce it? What is the best mix of our products and services to propose? What is the best price to charge? What values will the customer receive in return?

"So it's like going back to school?" the representative asks the manager. "I do my homework before going to class for the first time—and that solves the problem of overselling?"

"Let's put it this way," the manager explains. "It solves the problems of underknowing new markets and underdaring to move into them. If you take care of those two things, overselling in our mature markets will take care of itself."

"That's a nice undersold way to make your point."

How Do Customers Really Use Your Products? They May Know How to Sell Them Better Than You Do

"When was the last time one of my people asked one of your people how they use our product?" the sales manager asks the customer.

"*Ask* our people?" the customer says with surprise. "Ever since you renamed them 'applications consultants,' they don't ask much of anything. They *tell* our people how to use your product."

Ask yourself the same question: Do your salespeople regularly try to find out from customers how your product is being used? Do they know how it is applied, what new uses have been found for it, what procedures have been invented to optimize its performance or maintenance, what improvements have been made in it, what deficiencies have been corrected, what other products it may have been combined with to create systems? If you're not learning the answers to these questions on a consistent basis, you're probably missing something: new profits.

There is no doubt about it. You should be the expert on how your product is used. But often a manufacturer is the authority only on how his product is made and how it performs in ordinary recommended use. His customers become expert by themselves in the truly custom-tailored uses that could warrant premium prices to the manufacturer—if he knew.

When the head of a baking-mix manufacturer runs a nationwide bake-off contest for new uses of his product, what is the objective? No, it is not publicity, even though he receives a lot of it. His objective is to learn new ways that his customers use his product that will stimulate his staff to create new products, new ingredients, new recipes, and new advertising appeals.

When the top marketing executive at a process-controls manufacturer or an industrial valve company goes back over year-ago sales to see how the products that were bought from him are being used, is he seeking pats on the back or replacement business? He may get some of both. But his main interest is to find out what his customers have done with the product since they bought it. What have they learned about how to get the greatest value out of it? "Sure, I'm in the applications business," one manufacturer likes to say. "But my customers are in the business I apply myself to. I come at it from the outside. They're *in* it."

When manufacturers go back to their customers, what do they find? One dry-cereal manufacturer found that the department head of a large supermarket chain had come up with a plan-o-gram for shelving products that generated more profits than the manufacturer's plan did. A computer graphics company discovered a new market segment when it learned exactly who was using graphic displays inside the major companies of a key industry. AT&T uncovered some innovative uses for its telephone marketing strategies. A major chemicals processor learned how distributors were using its formulation recommendations as a selling tool instead of just a manufacturing guide.

No matter how much a seller knows about the processes or functions of his customers, all of them know something that few manufacturers know: the peculiarities of their own operations. This is what they are really expert at. You sell and install. Afterwards, they implement.

The vice president of operations for a large technical company torments all his suppliers by telling them, "We consider what we buy from you to be *raw materials*. You think they're finished goods. We regard them as raw until we get our hands on them and fit them to our needs. That's when they become finished—when we finish them." When his suppliers complain to him about being lowballed on price by his company, he tells them, "When *we* add the value, *we* keep the premium for ourselves. That's the price you pay for being a raw materials vendor."

What kind of procedure can you set up to make sure that you are taking advantage of your customers' proven propensity to invent your next sales opportunities? A number of suppliers are adopting a three-point approach:
  • At the time a sale is made, schedule regular trips to the

customer's plant to study the implementation of your product and its program of operations. One manufacturer refers to this as guaranteeing your "visitation rights."

• Get to know who the actual users of your product will be once it is installed and functioning in a customer's business. These people may not be at the buying negotiations, either as decision makers or as overt influencers. But they are the ones most likely to do the inventing on your product.

• Build an information bank on the ways customers alter, add to, amplify, supplement, and systemize your product on a use-by-use basis. Work with customers to determine the contributions these changes make to customer performance and cost-control results. Use the information in your database to fertilize your product development people, your advertising and sales-support staffs, and of course, your applications sales representatives.

"What makes us so smart?" a sales manager asks rhetorically. "We have smart customers. They pick up where we used to leave off. Now we're doing the picking up ourselves. We're picking up new profits as a result."

Instead of Knocking Your Head Against a Customer's Wall, Try Having a Nice Quiet Talk with Your Database

"I'm having trouble figuring out which way is best to enter my accounts," the sales representative says. "Should I get in wherever I can and sell what I can, or should I hold off until I get the opportunity I really want to make a major sale?"

His manager responds. "We like a short selling cycle here. Whichever way gets us the business first is the way to go."

"What bothers me is that the business I get early is almost always small potatoes or a larger-volume order at low margins," says the representative. "Neither of those situations does much for our profits, does it?"

"Nor does waiting around for the big score that never comes," concludes the manager firmly.

Which is better sales strategy: a little profit now or the chance of greater profit later? The question has been around a long time, but now, thanks to modern technology, initial entry and superior earnings can be one and the same.

The solution comes in the form of a database. It is stocked with information on important problems currently going on inside a customer's business, problems that the seller can help solve. The database contains information in the following categories:

1. A definition of each major problem.
2. Its location in the customer's business.
3. Its relation to the function or process in the customer's business of which it is a part.
4. Its contribution to cost.

5. The cost of the customer's current attempt to solve the problem.
6. The current solution's value in reducing the cost.
7. The nature of the *seller's* best solution, its cost, and the contribution it can make to solving the customer's problem.

This type of information brings the customer's business into focus. It enables a sales representative to see the big picture of his opportunity at the very outset of working with a customer. His major entry points are pinpointed for him so that he knows where to go for the greatest rewards. What's more, his manager knows where every sales representative should be directing his resources and can monitor performance against opportunity by using the same database his sales force uses.

This type of database can be as simple as a system of soapboxes organized in sequence to contain customer information in each of the seven categories. Or it can be computerized into an automatic system that each key account representative can operate with a portable terminal from his office, home, or anywhere on the road where there is an electrical outlet. Either way, the representative can get into a customer's business, study its problems, and plan how to solve them before he ever sets foot in the door.

Eavesdropping on a sales representative communicating with his database might sound something like this:

"Database, let me see the major problems we know about in this particular division of my customer. All right, out of that list of ten problems, give me a closer look at this one. I want to learn how it is expressed in the customer's own terms. Then I'd like to see exactly where it is located in the division's organizational structure, what kind of operation it is part of, and what the relationship is between that operation and the rest of the division's business. If you have a diagram of the process that it's embedded in or a flowchart showing how the stages of the operation are connected to each other, I'd like to see that too.

"Now let's get to the numbers. What does this entire process I'm looking at contribute to the division's total cost structure? Let me zero in on that total cost. How much does this specific problem contribute to it? That cost will be my sales target. The solution I must come up with will need to reduce that cost or maybe eliminate it altogether.

"I'd like to see what the customer himself is doing right now to solve the problem. What product or equipment is he using? From whom did he buy it? What did it cost? How much of a contribution is it making?

"What would my company's best solution consist of? How much would it cost? What would its contribution be toward solving the problem? Is it better than the customer's current solution? If so, by how much? That number is very important to me because I will base my price on it."

From what the sales representative learns by exploring his database, he can prepare his proposal to define the customer's problem and his solution of it in qualified terms: on the basis of the dollars to be saved in the customer's business and their value in net profit.

Where does the information in the sales representative's database come from? There are three main sources:

1. Information already in the files of his sales department.
2. Information that can be obtained from the customer.
3. Information available about the customer's business from public sources such as the annual report, the 10-K report, security analyst reports, trade association records, trade press articles, and government publications.

Instead of asking "How can I help you?" or "Which of your problems can I help you with?" the sales representative can take charge of his entry into his customer's business. "This is the problem I've chosen to study in your business," he can say. "Here is my understanding of how it affects your profits. I'd like you to compare that with the improved contribution it can make as a result of my solution."

This lets the representative enter a company where he can make the most money for his customer and for his own company. It gives him the opportunity to make a major sale and still allows his manager to say, "We like a short selling cycle here."

Either You're Selling Information That Helps a Customer Do Business Better, or You're Not Selling Anything at All

Because selling is one of the world's oldest vocations, it is filled with myths, and myths die hard. For example, many sales executives still believe that customers buy *products,* want *products,* need *products* and that the way to sell is therefore to sell *products.* Yet when sales representatives follow this ancient prescription, what happens? They end up not selling products at all but selling price. No one wants products, they conclude. All the customer wants is price. In this way, sales executives perpetuate two myths, neither of which will help any company make money in the 1980s or 1990s.

"If there's no market for products or services and there's no market for price, then there's no market, period," the sales representative says. "Right?"

"Wrong," the manager replies. "There's a market out there for something. All you have to do is figure out what. And if you can do it before the other guys, you may have the market all to yourself until they catch on. Then you can continue to dominate the market unless you let them catch up. How would you like a product line like that?"

Sales forces that sell products almost all have the same experience. They charge for the product and are forced to give away free services. The most necessary service is applications information—how the customer can integrate the product into his operations in the most cost-effective manner. Therefore, applications know-how is the key to extracting the full measure of value from a product. Without the knowledge of how to use the product, maintain it, and upgrade its performance, the product itself may be valueless, or at least considerably diminished in its ability to deliver benefits.

"Are you saying that what I'm really selling is how-to knowledge?" the representative asks. "Do you mean that all the stuff I carry around in my sample case, the stuff that all our brochures and catalogues describe, the stuff my quota and bonus are based on, is not what I'm really selling at all?"

"That's what I'm saying," the manager replies. "No matter how you slice it, you are either selling the best available information on how customers can solve the problems that we are very good at solving, or you are not selling anything at all."

"But it is still the product that makes the information work, isn't it?"

"Try it the other way around: it is the information that makes the product work."

Sales forces that have put their selling pressure against products for decades may have a hard time understanding why the egg called information must precede the chicken called the product. The best way to make the point may be by drawing an analogy.

"I once met a man who sold fertilizer," the manager says. "It was quality fertilizer, the highest, he told me. Since it was the best, I assumed he had the largest share of market and the highest profit on sales. When I told him that, he laughed. 'Unfortunately,' he said, 'the only correlation is an inverse one. Our margins have a hard time trying to recover the costs associated with maintaining our quality.' "

"Sounds like us," says the representative. "I must admit that many times I've thought of our product as a form of, shall we say, fertilizer."

The manager continues his story. "I told the fertilizer man, 'If you have such a problem selling that product, why not try giving it away? Suppose you were to pick a major farm customer and pleasantly surprise him by delivering a dozen truckloads of fertilizer to him absolutely free?' 'Pleasantly surprise him?' the man asked me. 'Quite the opposite. He'd be puzzled, not by what I did but by what he was going to do. And the more he thought about it, the madder he'd get. Finally, he'd tell me to come and get my fertilizer off his farm or he'd sue me.' I was surprised at this man's words at first, but I shouldn't have been. Why do you think a customer would react that way to a free sample?"

"He wouldn't know what to do with it."

"Right," says the manager, "so I made a second suggestion. 'Instead of giving away your fertilizer,' I said, 'how about giving away your knowledge about how to use it to make the maximum improvements in crop yield for the farm's particular soil, climate, and operating conditions? Suppose you dumped *that* on the customer?' I've forgotten the man's exact response, but what do you think a big farm customer would do then?"

"Maybe," the sales representative says, "he'd order some fertilizer to put the information to work . . . to get the increased yield."

Products don't solve problems any more than fertilizer grows crops. Information solves problems. Products and the people who sell them are implementers of information. The sales strategies of the 1980s are becoming increasingly databased in recognition of this fact. With top-notch data on customer problems and their own solutions, sales representatives can help customers learn the most vital information of all: how to apply products and services to improve customer profits.

"If information is the key to sales, then I'm doing it backwards," the representative says. "I should be studying my customers' businesses, not product performance specifications. Our new presentations should show the financial effects of applying our products and know-how to the customer's business problems. Our image in the marketplace should be as customer analysts and—what should I call it?—business benefiters. As a matter of fact, if our information is so valuable, is there any reason why we can't begin to charge for it?"

"Very interesting," the manager says. "Now I have some information for you. Try to remember all those things when you take over this region next Monday."

In the Midst of Probing for the Customer's Hidden Needs, Don't Miss the Needs Written All Over His Face

"You may think that customers guard their pocketbooks with their lives," the sales manager tells the representative as he takes a seat. "But there's something they sit on even harder: their true needs. They'll share some with you, but they're on the surface. It is the hidden needs they won't talk about that we need to know. That is the heart of selling: knowing a customer's hidden needs."

"Why won't they tell us?" the representative asks. "After all, they know we're there to help them. What's the big secret?"

The question seems so simple, but the sales manager knows he has opened the door to one of the most sensitive areas in selling. Needs reveal. They reveal where a business is weak, where it feels threatened, and where it fears it can be beaten out by competition. Needs provide competitive intelligence, and for that reason, many companies treat them as proprietary information. If they tell a supplier, it can become public overnight. Wants are something else. Wants are things to grow by. But needs are more vital, are more urgent, and have much more bearing on the current state of the business's health.

The sales manager does his best to explain this to the representative and then asks, "How do you dig out those hidden needs?"

"I don't," says the representative.

"You don't? You don't penetrate your customer's hidden needs? That means you're leaving business on the table, just waiting for one of our competitors to come along and pick it up for the asking."

"I think it's the other way around," the representative says. "I think I'm getting the business for us precisely because I leave hidden needs alone. It is my competitors who are leaving the business for me

83

while they spend all their time penetrating down to the subbasement of the customer's needs. They're digging mineshafts. I'm mining coal."

"You are also violating one of the fundamental principles of sales strategy," the manager warns. "You are dealing with surface needs. There's nothing more dangerous or deceptive. There can't possibly be any truth to them."

"Truth is in sales, and I'm making the sales." The representative knows the manager will never rest until he tells him how, so he continues. "I think there's an essential truth about a customer's business: What you see is what you get. That is why my first question to a customer is always, 'How's business?' expressed in some specific way. For instance, I'll ask how shipments are going, how inventory in a specific product category is moving, how receivable collections are coming along, how a new market is opening up, or how productivity improvement is advancing in the plant.

"Most of the time, I'll get an answer. Usually it is pretty definite. The customer will say the company is falling behind last month, sales are ahead of projections, or there's not too much new to report. Even when customers won't talk, their body language tells me something. So does their silence."

"What does all this teach you?" the manager asks.

"Their problems, their opportunities. The two most important things I can learn."

"But what have you learned about their hidden needs? That's what I'm concerned about."

"When they tell me about where their problems are," the representative says, "they are telling me they have a need for a solution. When they tell me about an opportunity, they are telling me they have a need to push it as far and as fast as it can go. That is what an opportunity is—a search for a way to make the most of it. If you run a business, you can't have any truer needs than solving your most pressing problems and taking full advantage of fleeting opportunities."

The manager persists, saying, "But how do you know that there aren't hidden needs underneath the ones you develop, ones deeper down that really influence buying decisions?"

"I'm sure there are," the representative acknowledges. "But because they're deeper down, they're less urgent, rather than more. I call them underlying needs, the ones the customer will get around to someday. I'm interested in the overreaching needs that he must deal with right now."

"That's a nice play on words: underlying and overreaching," the manager says. "I still don't buy your belief that because they're on the top of the mind they're the true needs. It seems to me you have to do something more to qualify them."

"I do," says the representative. "I qualify them by quantifying them."

The sales manager fixes the representative with a stare. "First it was underlying vs. overreaching. Now it is qualifying by quantifying. Pray tell, exactly how do you qualify by quantifying? Isn't that a contradiction in terms?"

"When a customer tells me his answer to my question by giving me an overreaching need, I follow up immediately by asking him two 'how much' questions. For example, I'll ask, 'How much have new receivable collections improved? How much more would you like them to improve?' Or if its marketing, 'How much has share already grown? How much more would you like it to grow?' Then I sit down with the customer to put together my proposal to meet his needs, to help him get the improvements he tells me he has got to have."

"Quantifying the overreaching need," the sales manager muses aloud. "The true needs are up front, not hidden. If you keep drilling for hidden needs, somebody else will sell the true needs first. All very interesting. Let me ask you something. Would you believe in hidden needs if I told you that my own hidden need in having this discussion with you was to assess you for a regional manager's title? And as far as I'm concerned, you've got the job."

"Not really. You see, that was my overriding need in responding to you the way I have."

You Know a Lot, but Not Everything, About a Customer's Business: That's Your Starting Point for Learning the Rest

"We spent a small fortune reeducating you people to sell for higher margins," the sales manager says sternly. "We deliberately taught you to sell up at higher levels in your customer organizations so that you'd have an edge on the competition. And what happens? You just don't use it."

He stares at them. "I don't have a new product to give you. I can't let you debase price any more. I can't hand you a monopoly. So I give you the best tool I can: selling up, a financial sell to customer management. And you ignore it. Why? Do you like price competition so much that you don't want to avoid it even when you can?"

The district managers stare back at him. Finally one of them speaks up. "I tried it," he says. "I did just what we were trained to do. I went upstairs in a customer organization and sought out a manager. The representative on the account was with me. I told the customer we were here to do business differently, that we were going to cut out some of his costs instead of just selling him our product.

"He flattened us with one question. 'Oh yeah,' he said. 'All of a sudden you're going to cut our costs? Where have you been all this time while our costs have been climbing out of sight? All you've done is add to our problems by overpricing your products.'"

The sales manager wants to know what he said to that. "Nothing," the district manager answers. "What could I say? That, after years of being a vendor, all of a sudden we were experts in his costs beginning at nine o'clock that morning? Or that we'd known all along how to help him reduce costs in a couple of his major operations but we just hadn't done anything about it? Maybe I just should have said we were too busy overpricing our product, as he suggested. I left my pride there but at least we still have the account."

As companies make the transition from straight vendor selling—pushing the product's features, functions, and benefits at a price—to taking on a more consultative role with key customers where price can be based more on value, many of their sales managers and representatives run smack into this problem. If they could have done it all along, why didn't they? Have they been derelict? If they just got smart yesterday, how come? Have they become overnight geniuses in the customer's business? Without answers, the salespeople back off. It almost comes as a relief to some of them to go back down the hall and negotiate price once again with the purchasing agent.

"So what you're telling me," the sales manager says, "is that you couldn't find a way to say yes and no at the same time so that it made sense to the customer. You couldn't say 'Yes, we could have been working with you to cut your costs all along.' And you couldn't say, 'No, we haven't become experts overnight; we know a lot but we don't know everything. That's our point of departure with you. Let's take it from there.' You couldn't say that?"

The district managers are staring at him again. "Well," he says, "let me tell you why you'd better start getting comfortable with saying that. There's a worse alternative. I know, I just ran into it myself.

"I thought I'd try some upper-level selling myself. So I called on an account, a prospect I've wanted for some time. I got upstairs and said my piece: 'I'd like to do business with you on a consultative basis. I'd like to reduce some of your costs and, in that way, earn the right to keep more of our margins because I will be helping you to make more money as well.'

"They were nice about it. 'Too bad you weren't here a couple of months ago,' they said. 'We've already entered into that kind of relationship with one of your competitors.' "

Everybody was quiet now. " 'Well, that's no problem,' I said to them. 'We're just as good as they are, in many ways better. Why not give us a crack at it, too, and see who does the better job? No way you can lose that way, is there?'

"To my surprise, they said yes, there was a way they could lose.

'We regard our cost information as proprietary,' they told me. 'It required a great deal of soul-searching before we decided to release any of it to an outsider. We wouldn't feel comfortable having it in *two* people's hands right now. Besides, our people are pretty busy. As it is, it's an imposition on them to ask them to take their time and teach your competitor the inside information. I could never get them to go over that same information twice.'

" 'So how can we work with you in a consultative manner?' I asked them.

"They replied, 'Well, if you want to submit a proposal based on what you think you already know about our operations, we'll certainly entertain it. Of course, if your numbers are way off, you could lose credibility with our people and that might hurt you in the long run. Or you can wait and see how the other guys work out.'

" 'What if they fall flat?' I asked him. 'Would that give us an opening?'

" 'Not necessarily,' they said. 'It might take us a while before we trust another outsider enough to work with you in this way.'

" 'What if they succeed, then would that open things up for a second source like us?' I asked.

" 'Probably not. We'd be inclined to go around a second time with a proven supplier.'

"In exasperation, I almost shouted at them, 'Then how can we ever switch over from vending to you and start consulting?'

" 'Well,' they said, 'it's the way we told you: Too bad you weren't here a couple of months ago.' "

In consultative selling, there is rarely a need for multiple sources. One will do. For the outside suppliers, there is no assurance of ever getting the next order. The time may never come. As the sales manager later notes, "We may be locked out of doing anything but vending with that account forever."

Overcoming the hurdle of where-have-you-been-up-to-now is not only possible, it is necessary to avoid being frozen out of the best opportunities for improving margins by improving customer operations. "That's my message," the sales manager says. "And don't ask me what makes me so smart all of a sudden. The answer is much too simple: a competitor who got there first."

In a Commodity Business Where You Think You Know Everything by Now, What You Don't Know Will Fill a Database

Squeezed by both the rising cost of sales and pressure from top management to improve profits on every sale, more and more sales managers are becoming keyed up about key accounts. In other words, they are rediscovering the 80-20 rule. If as much as 80% of profitable sales volume comes from as few as 20% of all accounts, alert sales executives are saying, the customers who make up that 20% should become the bull's-eye of our sales target.

As soon as this fact is out on the table, the next question is, "How well do we know our key account customers?" The first answer, the easy one, is almost always wrong: "Like the backs of our hands." The second answer comes a lot harder but it is a good deal more correct: "Not nearly well enough, if we really want to zero in on these accounts and base the achievement of 80% of our sales goals on them."

One of the most instructive exercises a sales manager can put his field force through is a key account needs inventory. This makes clear just what each salesman knows and doesn't know about his key accounts and the major decision makers in their midst.

A short while ago, a 25-man industrial division's sales force went through what experience has shown to be a typical inventory. The salesmen were told to "let it all hang out," and that produced some absorbing dialogue. First, look at the questions posed to Salesman A and see how he answers:

Q. Who is the key decision maker on the account?
A. Mr. Fred Smith, the purchasing agent.
Q. How long have you called on him?
A. Four years plus.

Q. What are the main subjects of your conversations with him when you call?

A. The Little League baseball team he manages.

Q. What does he reveal as his primary needs?

A. He wants me to act as his warehouse. And keep the price down.

Q. What unfulfilled expectations of you does he seem to have?

A. He wants more service than I can give him. Just to provide what I do is at times difficult.

Q. How do you plan to increase this account's profit contribution?

A. My overriding goal is to hang onto our current position.

Now Salesman B speaks out—in terms that are all too familiar to anyone who's been in sales management for a while:

Q. Who is the key decision maker on the account?

A. Mr. Bob Jones, director of corporate purchasing.

Q. How long have you called on him?

A. Five, six years or so.

Q. What are the main subjects of your conversations with him when you call?

A. He is a home gardener. His great pride in life is his green thumb.

Q. What does he reveal as his primary needs?

A. He wants economy. Savings, savings, savings. Price, price, price.

Q. What unfulfilled expectations of you does he seem to have?

A. He wants assurance all the time that I am giving him the greatest savings possible. Every time he signs an order, he feels he is laying his career on the line.

Q. How do you plan to increase this account's profit contribution?

A. By acting with extreme caution, inch by inch.

Finally, let's hear from Salesman C, who is quite frank about the sales problems he faces every day:

Q. Who is the key decision maker on the account?

A. Mr. George Brown, general manager and head buyer.

Q. How long have you called on him?

A. Ten years.

Q. What are the main subjects of your conversations with him when you call?

A. Women, horse racing, golfing, and new drinks.

Q. What does he reveal as his primary needs?

A. To be able to assure his plant superintendents that they will never be out of stock on our items.

Q. What unfulfilled expectations of you does he seem to have?

A. He always is interested in testing and evaluating new products. He wants me to pick up every new competitive product I can and bring it to him, as if I were his comparison shopper.

Q. How do you plan to increase this account's profit contribution?

A. By killing myself to ensure delivery within 48 hours, seven days a week, and eating the cost of the secondary stock warehouse I have to keep to do it.

It doesn't take an in-depth analysis of these salesmen's reports to realize several things. First, the business they are in is apparently a commodity business. Few if any competitive product differences exist, and buying is often based on price and delivery considerations. Second, the salesman-customer relationships seem to have become perfunctory. Little if any need prospecting is going on. Nor does there seem to be much penetration of accounts to reach a full roster of decision makers or buying influences. Third, no true penetration planning that could increase profitable sales is going on. All these factors can be found in any business. They are especially common to commodity businesses. Unfortunately, they also act to ensure that a commodity business remains that way.

Sales managers are coming to realize that the knowledge their sales forces have about key account needs can be the most important aspect of information resources. The problems are twofold: what the information should consist of and how it can be obtained.

Some companies are setting up a central audit of key account needs. Each need is carefully spelled out and evaluated for its intensity and potential growth. It is then restated in terms of the way the customer views this particular problem. A recommendation is made on how to solve each problem by prescribing the remedy of equipment and services that will yield an optimal profit for the supplier.

The key account audit is run like a blood bank. Only salesmen who deposit information can draw from it. "We treat it like blood," one sales manager says, "because knowledge of key account needs is our lifeblood." The bank contains information on key decision makers' hobbies and personal interests, of course. This is regarded as the "small change." The "big bills" are in the form of valid customer problems. These are the input that pay off.

In another company committed to systems sales, a four-source pipeline for key account information has been set up to keep its needs inventory well stocked. The sales force is required to file a monthly intelligence report on key customer needs that can lead to equipment sales and service sales, or to systems sales, which combine both equipment and services. Another report provides an opportunity for the sales force to file information on customer needs gathered from competitive sources, trade shows, and exhibits.

Finally, each salesman must file a monthly reading of customer-need information gathered from the general press, his own trade publications, and customer industry publications.

A company that takes its key accounts seriously is committed to maintaining a key account needs inventory as its most important product. The buyer's traditional question, "What's new?" for the first time may provoke a substantial answer. "These are the new key customer needs I am anticipating," a salesman may say. "These are the problems they can be translated into. And these are the new solutions I can prescribe to solve them and, in that way, earn more profitable sales volume for us."

Only when his people are capable of this sort of response can a sales manager say with assurance, "Yes, we know our key accounts."

What's Your Best Choice for Replacing a Sales Rep—or Giving a Rep the Best Partner a Man or Woman Can Have?

"I thought there were going to be four of us," the representative says. "Where are the other two?"

"We're all here," his manager replies. "Let's get the meeting started."

"I don't understand. You said I'd be introduced to my replacement and to my new teammate. Where are they?"

The manager smiles. He points to a red telephone. "Your replacement." Then he waves at a new minicomputer terminal. "Your new teammate," he says.

Meetings like this are taking place with increasing frequency between managers and their key account representatives. They are a sign of the times, reflecting (1) the economic revolution that in many cases is making the personal sales call unaffordable and (2) the technological revolution that is providing sales representatives with new forms of information support.

"I never heard of a telephone making a sale," says the representative. "How is this one going to replace me?"

"You're right. But sales representatives make sales when they use the telephone. I want you to make sales on this phone from now on instead of making personal calls on our Class C accounts—all of them, without exception. Before the year is out, you'll be using the phone for most of our Class B accounts as well."

"How will we sell them just by using the phone? That's pretty competitive business, you know."

"It's so competitive that we can't compete for it anymore. At least not at the cost of personal sales to major accounts. We're not the only ones. Our competitors are in the same position. We've all been out there buying unprofitable volume. No more. With the lower cost of selling on the phone, we may be able to make a profit when we make a sale." The manager pauses for effect.

"But what about my quota?" the representative asks. "That's based on my sales presence—my personality, my persuasiveness—all the things you hired me for."

"They'll come across over the phone. But if you stop and think about what you've been doing with your Class C and B accounts, how much has really depended on persuasive selling? Mostly, you've been taking orders—the same order and reorders over and over again. Repeat business, right? The only thing that's different is that now I want you to get it over the phone."

"What about the rest of the time when I've been fighting tooth and nail for the business? How much of that business am I going to be able to retain?"

"More than I'm happy with, I'm afraid," responds the manager. "Those are the sales we hardly ever make money on. Much of the time we lose money. I'm afraid you'll still get your share. But I hope you'll leave a lot of them to our friendly rivals."

The representative seems confused. Even surprised. "So much for my replacement. I'll have a telephone bill now instead of gas bills, tolls, and hotels. Now you're going to give me another machine for a teammate?"

"They have a lot in common. Each is designed to be a multiplier for you. The telephone will extend your range, let you cover dozens more customers than you ever could in person. Now your new partner, the minicomputer, will multiply your knowledge of key account sales opportunities where the big profits are—for the customer and for us."

"What's in the computer that's going to make me want to team up with it?"

"Two things. One is a database on each of your major customers' problems. The database will steer you directly to the most profitable problems for you to solve. It will also match them up with the best solutions we have to solve them. How's that for a teammate?"

"Sounds O.K. so far. But what do I have to do in return?"

"Feed it. Supply it with new information on customer problems. Stock it with new information on customer decision makers. Stuff it with new information on our solutions and their benefits. That way, it will always be 'user-friendly' to you."

"I don't mean to sound greedy," the representative says, "but can I count on my teammate for anything else, or is that it?"

"The best is yet to come. Your new teammate has a printer attached. After you've analyzed a customer problem and worked out the most profitable solution to it, your teammate will type out your proposal for you. That means all the words and figures, ready to present to the customer just as they come out of the machine."

The representative leaves the meeting with his two new associates and begins a different style of selling. It is not long before he discovers that he can use the time saved by calling minor accounts on the telephone to increase the hours he can apply to higher-profit customers. Periodically, he will supplement the telephone with direct mail, but the focus remains on his Class A customers, where the time invested will pay off.

What next? The answer is already in the works: a computerized reorder system for repeat purchases that will reduce time on the telephone and allow it to be used for selling, not order taking.

If there is a wave of the future, its trend is clear. Sales representatives should sell, sales managers should manage, and customers should be sources of profit.

In Order to Bank on Sales, First Bank Customer Data

"Nothing that sales management does costs more than collecting and distributing information, unless it is the penalty for not doing it." This quote from a general sales manager is both a common complaint in most companies today and a recognition of how centrally important having the facts has become. Managers long ago came to realize that there is no substitute for sales information—that is, information from the field about what is going on out there.

Lately, there has been a growing awareness that information is a two-way process. Discussions are taking place among many sales and marketing people in a wide range of consumer, industrial, and service companies who are asking such questions as:

1. How can information serve a salesman in the field or his manager?
2. What kind of information is most useful?
3. What would salesmen do with this information if they had it?
4. What type of system should my company set up to acquire and distribute this information?

There are no pat answers to these questions. Nonetheless, certain generalizations may be made as guidelines for setting up a sales force information program that can be operated with minimal waste motion. Let's look at each of these in detail.

1. Information's purpose: decision assistance. The most significant question to ask about information is, "What would you do with it if you had it?" The best answer is, "Make better decisions." Better decision making (and "better" means "more likely to improve profitable sales volume") is the ultimate rationale for incurring the

96

costs, both human and financial, of setting up an information system for field salesmen. Some say it is the *only* reason.

To help salesmen improve the quality of their decisions in the field, companies are setting up multiple information banks. These are often referred to as decision-assistance information systems. Some are completely computerized, providing portable terminals that give regional managers or even field salesmen direct access to a central data storage bank. Others may be partially programmed for a computer but otherwise retrieve data manually. No matter what the technical aspects of storing and gaining access to the information may be, the overriding consideration is that data must flow quickly, regularly, and accurately to the sales force, where they can be put to work in making better decisions.

What types of decisions are salesmen likely to improve if they're literally plugged into corporate headquarters? Companies exploring answers to this question have identified such subjects as:

- "How am I doing? What should I do to improve my perform-ance? How do I compare with the rest of our sales force?"
- "How is my competition doing? What is it likely to do next? If it's doing better than I am, why?"
- "What are the major needs of my key accounts that I should zero in on to maximize my efforts?"
- "What are the major needs of my key accounts' customers? How can I help my accounts serve their own customers better by using my products and services?"
- "What is the economic outlook in my industry, in my cus-tomers' industry, and in my customers' customers' industries? Also, what social and political factors may influence their needs, the way they do business with me, and my sales?"

2. Data that any sales force needs. Most companies are experienced in giving data to their salesmen in such forms as pricing guidelines, gentle prods to explore new applications for products, and warnings of zigzags in the economic outlook. More recently, companies have begun to fertilize their sales forces on a regular basis with three additional types of information: about (1) each salesman's performance; (2) competitive performance, products, and strategies;

and (3) key customers' needs and business prospects. Data are bundled together at weekly intervals and sent to the field in the form of a decision-assistance information pack.

Some of its major components usually include:

Salesman performance information—a summary of how each salesman is performing against his quota, overall and according to a product-by-product, account-by-account analysis. The record is kept current on a weekly basis and totalled every month or quarter. Information can also be included to allow each salesman to compare his performance with fellow salesmen's, with his previous record, and with his current expectations against budget.

Competitive performance information—an evaluation of how competition is performing overall as well as on a product-by-product, account-by-account schedule (when these facts are known). This competitive record can also be kept as up to date as the salesman's. If possible, a territorial breakout is included to show each salesman the specific effects of competitive performance in his area. When competitive strategies can be anticipated, they also are integrated into the performance record.

Customer performance information—an analysis of the needs of key customers that is designed to help capture more of their business. A running examination of the business situation faced by each salesman's key accounts can be included in the same bundle, as well as each account's relevant social, economic, political, and technological context. As customer information builds up, scenarios may be put together on all of the company's important customers. These may be compiled into a source book for salesmen who currently serve the accounts and for salesmen who will come into them in the future.

3. Keep the first system simple. For sales managers whose problem is, "How can we get started?" a system can be constructed from a mix of information on hand, supplementary facts in the public domain, and the gradual infusion of new data. The first step is to set objectives. The major goal of an initial information system, of course, is to improve the quality of short-term decision making by sales management and salesmen with respect to field practices and policies that affect profitable sales volume. Be sure to limit the focus of each objective so that you can concentrate on a single area at a time.

Next, get into action to achieve the systems' objective. A six-phase program can be designed along the following lines:

1. Make a model of the field sales environment so that the major decision areas stand out clearly.
2. Identify the critical data requirements that affect the quality of decision making in each major area. These data will become the system's "software." They generally include information about market needs, competitive activities, and product performance characteristics.
3. Make a comparative rating of the relative availability of the data required. Identify all the types of data that are crucial but not readily available.
4. Put together two companion feedlines. One will carry the currently available data to the field; the other, data that are not yet readily obtainable. Go to work filling the first line and pipe it through to the field. At the same time, fill in the second line.
5. Combine the two feedlines into a single system. Have it structured into an organized flow, and identify its hardware requirements and data processing procedures.
6. Create a periodic newsletter to supplement the flow of information to the field. Provide room in it for comments and even contradictory data to be contributed by the salesmen.

The simple system approach will put any company in the sales force information business quickly and at relatively low cost. Any program worth its salt should begin to pay for itself almost at once and should continue to amortize its investment many times throughout its lifetime. It ought to be a major influence on improving the profitability of sales decisions, as well as a prime source of support for the salesmen's efforts to educate their customers.

Sorry, No More Well-Rounded Salespeople—Only Pointed People Need Apply

After all the talk about selling being multidimensional, it turns out that there is only one dimension to it—the size of the improvement you can make in the customer's profits.

Field sales manager (addressing a group of sales recruits): You people may not realize it, but you just missed a great nonexperience: being trained as well-rounded sales representatives. By "well-rounded" I mean people trained to marshal an endless collection of complex skills, activities, and information, and then adapt them to every customer's individual needs. Well-rounded salespeople were supposed to be adept at such things as listening, reading, asking, planning and strategizing, communicating, managing time, overcoming objections, knowing their products, and understanding markets. They were truly multidimensional men and women. Well, you won't catch me trying to turn out that sort of sales representative any more.

1st sales recruit: What's wrong with being well-rounded?

Manager: Two things. First, it's impossible. No one can ever achieve it. You end up with a lot of rough-edged, partially knowledgeable people smoothed over with a gloss of arrogance because they fancy themselves to be rounded. Now, you may argue that point with me, but the second reason makes the argument academic: Well-rounded people can't sell as effectively as pointed people.

2nd recruit: What's a pointed person? Someone who scores points with the customer?

Manager: A pointed person has been honed to a fine point, not stuffed to roundedness with training in every skill that can be imparted and a lot more that can't. A pointed person is deliberately one-dimensional.

3rd recruit: What's the one dimension?

Manager: It's the skill of selling in ways that help customers improve their bottom line. A pointed person is obsessed with customer profit improvement as his one true sales mission.

3rd recruit: Why is that? Why that obsession and not any one of a dozen others?

Manager: Because a pointed person believes that the principal effect a sales representative must have on a customer is *economic.* That leads right to concentrating on customer moneymaking.

1st recruit: Don't you have to listen to your customer to help him make more money from doing business with you? Don't you have to ask questions, read, plan, and do all the other things you said you weren't going to train us to do?

Manager: Yes. But just because you need to do all those things doesn't mean that you must be trained in them. I'm going to take a calculated risk. I'm going to assume that you probably listen and ask questions reasonably well right now—certainly well enough to act intelligently with a customer. So I want to concentrate on filling your heads with the *right questions.* Then I want to equip you with the *right answers.*

2nd recruit: Suppose we learn the right questions but express them badly? Or suppose we don't know how or when to listen and we miss an answer?

Manager: I'll chance your expressing yourselves badly, not writing better reports, or not flowing gracefully through a presentation. You can even have a tin ear for a lot of what's said as long as you listen to the answers to two questions. Anybody care to guess what they are?

1st recruit (after a full minute of silence): I guess we give up.

Manager: The two questions I want you to ask, and listen for the answers to, are designed to get at the heart of the customer's business—at least the heart as far as your role with him is concerned. Their purpose is to open up your selling opportunity to him in the most revealing way and do it on his own terms.

3rd recruit: What do you want us to ask?

Manager: You get at the first question by saying, "Mr. Customer, I'm out after your costs. Wherever my products and services can reduce them, I want to bring them down. So tell me, where are they?" That's No. 1. Question No. 2 is different: "Mr. Customer, I want to step up your sales. Wherever my products and services can boost your revenues, I want to raise them. Tell me why your customers buy from you. How can I help you sell them even more?"

1st recruit: Why are those the questions a pointed person asks?

Manager: Because they're pointed at the solar plexus of every customer's main concern: his profit. The answers to those two questions will tell you the only ways that profits can be improved.

2nd recruit: But they don't even mention our products.

Manager: Our products are meaningless! Think about it for a minute. What does our product represent to us? It's a cost, that's what it is. A cost to make and a cost to sell. And what does the product represent to our customer? The same thing: a cost. A cost to buy and a cost to use. So what is the right way to measure the value of our product? Only as a contributor to reducing a customer's other costs or increasing his sales. That's the only way he can justify paying our price.

3rd recruit: That's another thing: Your pointed questions don't say anything about price, either.

Manager: Price is meaningless, too, unless the customer perceives that he will receive a greater value in improved profit than the investment he must make. This is basic cost-benefit thinking. In that sense, our price is important only in relation to the profits it generates for your customer once he is committed to your product.

1st recruit: What about sales volume and share of market?

Manager: Volume means something to the customer only when he can see how a given volume of our product affects his sales and profit. As for market share, it means little unless the customer knows that a "share point" of his market is worth a specific number of profit dollars and that each additional point will return more profit than it costs to achieve.

2nd recruit: So if I'm going to be pointed, I need to ask the two pointed questions and listen, even badly, for the answers. Then what?

Manager: Then show how our products and services can lower costs and increase sales. Here again, you can make a poor presentation instead of a spellbinder. You can meet objections when you come across them instead of trying to overcome them.

3rd recruit: You want us to do two things perfectly—or pointedly, as you call it—and you could care less how proficient we become in everything else. As long as we point up customer profit improvement, we're doing our job and you'll be satisfied, right?

Manager: Right. Now do you understand my unrounded philosophy of training?

Recruits (in chorus): We get the point!

When They Cry for Help Out in the Field, Send Them a New Body—a Body of Information

The old-fashioned way to deal with markets is to throw bodies at them. Now it's become much more cost-effective to throw knowledge at them to add value to the bodies already out there.

Regional sales manager: Thanks but no thanks for the new salesman.

General sales manager: He's one of our best producers: good motivation, does his homework, customers love him. What's the problem?

Regional SM: It's not with the man. Right now I'd have a problem with anyone you'd send me. It's not what I need.

General SM: But you said you needed help. In our business, help traditionally comes in the form of bodies.

Regional SM: Maybe, but I don't think that holds true any longer. When I asked for help, I didn't want people-help; I wanted data-help.

General SM: Since when does data sell better than a salesperson?

Regional SM: Since our customers began to realize that their businesses are collections of problems and since we began to perceive our mission as helping to solve those problems.

General SM: Isn't that what our sales force has been trained to do?

Regional SM: The salesmen can't do a thing without data. That's why I need your help. We need a base of knowledge about our customer's businesses so that our people and their people can agree on how best to work together.

General SM: Up until now, we've been concentrating on

104

identifying our customer's decision makers and influencers; why they buy, from whom, at what price.

Regional SM: Now we need to know what their problems and costs are, and why they favor different solutions. That's what we don't have. Without it, we're just competitive. With it, we have our only chance to be out front.

General SM: If I give you that, you'll send the new salesman back to me?

Regional SM: By return mail. You see, that's exactly the trade-off today. Either we throw knowledge at our customers' problems or we throw bodies at them. I'm willing to subsidize your investment in customer information by keeping my staff lean.

General SM: Be careful. You may be giving away the ball game.

Regional SM: I don't think so. I'd rather have a slimmer staff that knows customer problems and how to solve them. I'll get more productivity per salesman, plus a much more exclusive position with my key accounts as their supplier of preference.

General SM: So you're telling me that if I spring for your database, you'll run a lower-cost operation to compensate for what I put up?

Regional SM: At first, yes. But very soon, I'll run a *higher sales* operation. My opportunities will increase to the point where we'll both be glad to increase the cost of capitalizing on them. As long as my contributions stay ahead of my costs, why worry?

General SM: My experience in this business tells me that you're posing an unstable situation. Costs always rise to equal revenues—and then exceed them. You'll be back to me for a second round of costs, won't you?

Regional SM: We'll have to update the database periodically, sure. But those costs will come out of revenues and should keep on paying for themselves. But you're right. There is one more type of cost I'll come back for.

General SM: I knew it. Go ahead, hit me.

Regional SM: My first request was for data about our customers' businesses that they know but we don't. My second request will be to learn where the problems are in our customers' businesses that *neither* of us knows enough about.

General SM: What sort of problems are those?

Regional SM: Exactly what they're selling and what they're not; where they're selling it and where they're not. Then who's selling it for them and who is not—what distributors, what retailers. How their agents are performing, outlet by outlet, product by product, customer by customer, price by price.

General SM: That's more than we know about our own business. How can we get this data; can we even afford it?

Regional SM: How do we get it? We work with our key accounts to set up a computerized system that's based on our customers' records. Both of us read the data while they're still hot. Then we zero in on the problems that we can help them with. We get the slow movers to move, provide their sales force with technical or even sales support, fill up their inventory where orders are outrunning deliveries. And where they're selling well, we make sure to step up our own deliveries.

General SM: Do those computerized systems exist?

Regional SM: Sure. They're on line right now in several industries. We're just lucky none of our competitors have done it to us yet.

General SM: So what if we're second? At least we'd know then that the system works in our industry and someone else will have the pleasure of debugging it.

Regional SM: That's another trade-off I'll gladly make. Give me the bugs that infest the leader! I'll take them in exchange for the opportunity that leadership gives me to form partnerships in problem solving with my major customers. If I do it right, I'll be side by side with my customers at the bottom of their learning curves. We'll rise together. Then let No. 2 in my industry try to squeeze me out! He'll never catch up with what I know.

General SM: Johnny-come-lately will be too late?

Regional SM: Right. That's the argument for getting in first. Maybe that's the third trade-off: time for money. I'd go for time. If we move fast, we can start making a return on our investment that much sooner.

General SM: You make it all sound so simple—and affordable. I guess that's why you're such a good salesman.

Regional SM: Credit it to the homework I've been doing on sales information systems. I'd be nowhere without my database.

4
Problem Solving

Working with the Customer to Improve His Business

The Best Way to Improve Sales May Be Simply to Stop Selling

Problem solving has become everybody's favorite definition of selling. Strangely enough, to solve customer problems you may actually have to stop selling.

Sales Representative: This isn't a sales call, really. I thought I'd just drop by today to mark the end of a way we've been doing business with each other—you know, say a few hails and farewells.

Customer: What's happening? You leaving the job, or getting out of selling, or what?

Representative: Actually, both of the above are true depending on how you define them. Yes, I'm leaving the job if you mean, Am I going to stop selling to you the way I have been? And yes, I'm getting out of selling if you mean, Am I not going to continue the traditional rituals that I've been going through on sales calls?

Customer: You're getting out of what you've been doing, but you're getting into something similar to it, is that what it's about?

Representative: Basically, yes. Essentially I will never again come in here and try to sell you on my products' features and benefits. And you will never again turn me away because of price.

Customer: That won't leave either of us much to talk about, will it?

Representative: Put it the other way. I don't think you and I have had very much to talk about in our traditional relationship. You know my product story almost as well as I do. When I go through it with you, are you really listening anymore? On my part, I know your price objectives practically down to the penny by now. We've spent a lot of time talking about them, but I don't think we've had much of substance to say for a very long time.

Customer: But what else is there for us to get involved in? It's your job to sell high and it's my job to buy low.

Representative: That's not my job anymore, remember? I'm

not selling anymore, at least not that way. That's why we'll have more things to talk about.

Customer: Like what?

Representative: Your business, that's what. Every time I come in here from today on, I'm going to have different pieces of paper to lay down in front of you. No specification sheets, no catalogues, no price lists, and no bids. Instead, I'll have descriptions of problems in your business operations and as much documentation as I can find to back them up.

Customer: What do you mean by *problems?*

Representative: A slow-moving product line in one region. An inventory buildup. Backordering. Order processing being unnecessarily slow and inefficient. Problems like that.

Customer: Where are you going to learn about them?

Representative: From a variety of sources. My own homework, for one, based on my contacts in the company. I'm going to read about your business—what you publish yourselves and what your own people write about in the trade press. The rest will come from a variety of outside sources. And then there's my main source.

Customer: What's that?

Representative: You.

Customer: Why will I be your main source?

Representative: Because it will be in your own best interest, that's why. The more information you and I share about what your company's problems are, the better we can help the company solve them. And that's the common denominator for both our jobs—solving the company's problems.

Customer: That's what I've always done. The company's main problem is making more money. That's why I keep an eagle eye on the price of everything we buy.

Representative: But both of us know it's not that simple. Low price doesn't always reduce cost best. There are many other factors involved in helping your company make more money. Our product's performance is one. How well we train your people to get full performance out of it is another. And how skilled we are in helping you maintain it in operation and upgrade it over time is yet another. If we do all those things well, problems that stand in the way of making more money will get solved faster and more economically.

Customer: I'm still not going to pay any more for a solution than I have to.

Representative: I won't expect you to. The price you pay for a solution will be based on what gives you the best solution in the fastest time. Let's call that the best price.

Customer: Let me see if I have all this straight. You're going to be a problem solver, not just a solution recommender. What if it works? What do we get then?

Representative: Credit for solving the problem.

Customer: Exactly. And then what do we do?

Representative: Find another problem to solve. And another, until we get in the habit of dealing only with priority projects that have the most impact on this company's profits.

Customer: Sounds good. Now how would you like to get started with me to solve our second problem?

Representative: Second? What was the first?

Customer: That we weren't going to devote ourselves to product and price anymore, remember. You did so well solving that one with me—we've set a high standard to try to match.

If Your Product Is Mature, a Me-Too Commodity, or Even Inferior, Relax . . . You've Got It Made

Very often, the worst kind of product to sell is the one with superior features and benefits. When that happens, it's only natural to sell the features and benefits and forget the customer.

Field sales manager: If you come to work for us, I can promise you a product line with three of the greatest selling advantages any salesperson could ask for. Would you care to guess what these advantages might be?

Sales representative: The first one has to be technical superiority—an innovation that's far better than anything the competition can offer.

Manager: No, quite the opposite. The best we have is parity with competition. We have a very good me-too product line. But there's nothing really innovative about it. After seven years on the market, it qualifies as mature.

Representative: Well, then it couldn't be inferior to our competitors' lines. If it can't be better, at least it can't be worse.

Manager: Sorry to contradict you again. But some entries in our line are regarded as inferior to some of our competitors' products. That's two out of two you've missed. Want to try for three?

Representative: The third has to be a complete line with everything the customer needs from one source.

Manager: That's three for three. Our line is far from complete. In fact, hardly a day goes by that we aren't made aware that some key elements are simply unavailable from us.

Representative: These are what you call the three greatest selling advantages I could ask for: me-too sameness, inferiority, and unavailability. All you need to add to that lineup is the highest price in the industry, and you'll have the greatest *disadvantages* a salesperson could ask for.

Manager: We do. Our price is the industry's highest. That's actually our fourth advantage.

Representative: When you think of the first three, I don't see how you can charge any price at all. You should be giving the line away—if you can find any takers. How can you call these things advantages? And why would anyone want to go to work selling for you?

Manager: Our entire sales success is based on the characteristics I've called our advantages. Oh, I admit that I sometimes feel the way you do and wish we had the product superiority, innovativeness, and a complete line. But I eventually feel glad that we don't.

Representative: We all have our moments of madness, I guess.

Manager: No, being glad occupies my rational moments. You see, if we had a superior, complete line, we'd probably be unable to resist the temptation to sell it. And that would be fatal.

Representative: Fatal? That would be paradise.

Manager: Paradise has proved fatal before, you know. I give you Adam. If we sold from superiority, what do you think would take place?

Representative: You'd have what a former sales manager of mine called "pride in product." You'd push product, product, product because you'd want everybody to be aware of its superiority.

Manager: Exactly. And what kind of orientation do you think we'd have as a result?

Representative: A product orientation, naturally.

Manager: And what would be the basis for our authority with the customer?

Representative: Your product knowledge. And taking it back to its source, technical knowledge of how to make the product, how to install it, and all that. The place would be crawling with technical bulletins.

Manager: Can you really visualize our advertising and sales literature?

Representative: Sure. Wiring diagrams, cutaway sections, performance specifications. Features and characteristics first, operating benefits second.

Manager: What do you think our competitors would be doing?

Representative: That's easy, too. Trying to convince the market that their benefits were just as good or better than yours. Coming out with new features, getting them knocked off, coming out with more new ones, and so on. The air would be filled with claims and counterclaims.

Manager: You see, we're free from all that. We can't talk features or operating benefits, so we don't. Our wiring diagrams look just like the other guys', so we let them show where the wires go. Our specs and their specs are virtually identical, so we feel there's no sense in doing much more than letting customers know we're on the approved list and letting it go at that.

Representative: If you don't talk about what everybody else talks about, what is there to say?

Manager: A lot. You can figure it out for yourself. If you can't find anything worthwhile to say about your own business, whose business would you want to talk about?

Representative: Your competitors'?

Manager: Try again.

Representative: What's left—your customers'?

Manager: Exactly. And what do you think you'd say?

Representative: I'd have to find out first what they're interested in. You can't talk to people unless they care about what you're saying.

Manager: Remember that, the next time you find yourself talking about *your* product, *your* services, *your* deals. But you still haven't answered the question. Without talking about what's yours, what could you discuss that's theirs?

Representative: *Their* business, *their* products, *their* problems—is that what you mean?

Manager: Yes, but what about them?

Representative: The difficulties they're having that we know about and that we're skilled in dealing with. Or we could turn it around and talk about potential new sales they might be able to gain if they did certain things that we could help them with. Use our products, for instance. And our expertise in applying them. I guess the easy way to say it is that we could learn where they're weak or hung up with heavy costs or inefficiencies. Or where they're strong and could become even stronger, and then help them in those areas.

Manager: Do you think they'd be interested in talking to us on that basis—would they find it important to have a meeting with us?

Representative: That's like asking if they'd find it important to solve their own problems. Of course. It wouldn't be just interesting for them to hear us out, but necessary if we really knew their business.

Manager: What about our product line—what role would that play?

Representative: Not a leading one, that's for sure. It would be part of the solutions we'd be selling. But that's just it—we'd be selling solutions to customer problems, not products. The product would have to make its contribution to the solutions we'd sell. But so would the services that go with it. And the support people in various specialities. And our financing plan. Our warranty program. How well we teach the customer's people to use what we sell. The product's a part of the whole solution, an important part. But it's not the whole solution by itself.

Manager: Suppose we were able to solve customer problems with packages like you've described—we call them "systems"? What kind of price do you think we could charge?

Representative: If you could solve expensive problems for a customer, he'd be willing to pay you an expensive price. In fact, almost any price that was cheaper than the cost of the problem would be a fair price. And in some cases—for instance, if you could help the customer open up a market that could give him millions of dollars in profits every year—your price could be whatever amount you make it.

Manager: Well, thanks for thinking things through with me. I've enjoyed it. I hope what we've talked about will come in handy for you when you find a company you'd like to work for—one that can give you the greatest selling advantages.

Representative: I've already found it.

It's Fine to Be a Problem Solver—It's Even Better if You Know the Problem

In sales, the relationship between cause and effect shows up fast. But the relationship between a problem and its symptoms—and a problem and its solution—is always much more obscure.

Sales representative: I hate to say this, but we've really let our competitors get a jump on us this time. They're getting a lot of attention with their new problem-solver campaign.

Field sales manager: How so?

Representative: Well, they're going to our customers and saying, "Sure, anybody can sell products; our mission is to help solve your problems. If you want to do business with a peddler, you can go anywhere. But when you want your problems solved, come to the problem solvers!"

Manager: What kind of reception are they getting?

Representative: Great! Everybody's throwing problems at them. They're swamped.

Manager: What kind of problems are they swamped with?

Representative: One that I know of is to design a new inventory control system. Another is to come up with a collection system for a customer's accounts receivable. A third is to come up with an order-entry system.

Manager: Is that how they're defining problems, in those words?

Representative: The exact words. Why?

Manager: Those are the names of systems, not problems. They're product-oriented terms. They refer to our own business as systems suppliers, not to our customers' business.

Representative: Why do you say that? Our customers have

116

inventory to control. They have receivables to collect from their customers. They have orders to enter. Aren't those problems?

Manager: Not in themselves, they're not. Take the accounts receivable situation. Notice I said *situation,* not *problem.* Anybody can collect receivables.

Representative: Not easily. Not quickly, at least not all the time. And not all of them. Even some that you eventually collect can cost you more than they're worth, to say nothing of the aggravation.

Manager: Now you're talking problems. Can you find a way to summarize what you just said?

Representative: Accounts receivable is a problem because it costs money. It can be expensive to live with if you don't solve it. And it can be expensive to solve, too.

Manager: So what kind of a problem is it, would you say?

Representative: O.K., it's a financial problem.

Manager: Let's keep thinking. What's the precise nature of the financial problem posed by uncollected receivables?

Representative: Well, a company goes out and sells something. That costs something. It makes the goods and ships them. That costs. Then it sits around and waits to get paid, sending out bills over and over again. That adds to the costs.

Manager: So what does an uncollected receivable represent?

Representative: A whole series of costs, one on top of the other. Then good money being thrown after bad.

Manager: What's the net effect of those costs?

Representative: They can cut into the profit on the original sale, can't they? As a matter of fact, they can wipe out profit completely.

Manager: So what kind of a problem does that present to a company?

Representative: It can't make the profit it planned to make— and deserves to make. It's almost as if it hadn't made the original sale in the first place.

Manager: Exactly. If you can't collect, you haven't sold. It's even worse, actually, because you're still saddled with all the costs of selling.

Representative: So a collection department that can't collect wipes out the sales department's best efforts. The company is working against itself.

Manager: From the customer's point of view, then, what is the problem?

Representative: "Help cut my costs from collections. Help guarantee the efforts of my sales department. Help me get my hands on the cash that my planners have budgeted for." The problems—the real problems, I mean—have nothing to do with receivables at all.

Manager: Don't ever forget what you just said. Now tell me, if you were going to solve these problems, what would the end objective of your solution have to be?

Representative: To help these people collect . . . no, that's wrong. To help the company improve its profit by reducing the amount of receivables outstanding and reducing the cost by which they're collected.

Manager: You didn't use the words *receivables collection system.* How come?

Representative: Because that's not the solution. It's not the problem, either.

Manager: What is it?

Representative: It's the means by which we, in our business, can bring about a solution. That's *our* problem, isn't it: to design a system and make it operate at the best cost-effectiveness? But the solution is new dollars for the customer. It has to be, because the problem is that current dollars are being drained away.

Manager: So, given that insight, what would you say to a customer with a receivables problem if you had only one sentence to open his mind?

Representative: "How would you like us to improve your profit on sales?" That's really what it's all about, isn't it?

Manager: Do you think that if you spoke that way, you'd be addressing the customer's problem; that if you could deliver on the implied promise, you'd help solve his problem?

Representative: Yes.

Manager: Do you think you'd have to tell him you were a problem solver or would he be able to tell?

Representative: He'd know just by the way I delivered the opener. And because he'd see I was really getting at the heart of the problem, he might see the difference between our approach and the way that competition is using the words *problem solver* without the substance.

Manager: By the way, what do you think about our competitors' approach now that we've discussed it?

Representative: I don't think they've defined the problem.

While You're So Busy Trial-Closing the Customer, Look Around: He May Be Trying to Close the Sale Himself

No sooner have the manager and his newest salesperson entered the customer's building than they come to a dead stop, just out of earshot of the receptionist. "One of the things I'm going to be paying very close attention to on this sales call is your closing technique," the manager says. "I'll be watching for your first trial close, then your second or third, and after that your final close. I hope you're confident about your competence in closing."

"I'm very confident," the young man says. "I don't have any competence at all in closing."

"You don't?" the manager almost shouts. "Then how do you ever close a sale?"

"I never do, I guess. I let the customer do the closing."

Few of the techniques of so-called professional selling skills receive as much attention as the close. It is a hot button of just about every sales manager. One of the long-prevailing myths of selling is that more sales get away because they aren't closed properly than for any other single reason—except, perhaps, because they aren't opened properly, or at all.

In some sales forces, the pressure to close quickly is so extreme that the ideal presentation might be something like this: "Good morning. How many and when? Would you like to sign here?" But in major sales where the customer must play more than an order giver's role—where he must truly participate as an equal partner—what is the proper role of closing techniques? Whose province are they—the salesperson's or the customer's?

"You must have very obliging customers," the manager says. "To do your work for you like that, they must all be relatives. Why would any customer in his right mind close your sale for you?"

"Because it's his sale, too," the man replies. "He wants the values I represent as much as I want him to have them. When he has a clear understanding of them and sees how they can help him, then he is ready to buy. Until then, he isn't and he shouldn't."

"You can lead a horse to water, you know, but you can't make him drink by just standing there until he gets thirsty," the manager says. "You've got to put his head in the water. How many situations do you have right now where your customers are just standing around admiring themselves in the reflection of the water?"

"A few. But most of them eventually drink. My hit ratio, in fact, is a lot better on major sales when I let the customer close than it used to be when I tried to trial-close him every sentence or two."

"Aha!" says the manager. "You said the magic word: *eventually*. Most of them *eventually* buy. Just how long is eventually? Do you think the factory can just sit around forever waiting for your eventual sales? Do you think our competitors are going to cool their heels in the waiting room, patiently reading last month's magazines, to give you the time you need to close an eventual sale? Do you think our forecasting and inventory people have some privileged insight into your eventual timetable so they can schedule eventual production to meet your eventual orders?"

"My *eventually* isn't a long time. I sell much larger orders, and at much more profitable margins, when I let the customer close at the end of an hour, or even on a second call, than when I used to try for a wham-bam close. He knows that his own self-interest is involved, not just mine. I'd rather spend the time making that clear to him than trying to commit him before he's ready."

"But how do you know he's ready if you don't try to close him?" the manager asks. "He may be ready long before he gets around to letting you know."

"There are lots of ways my customers let me know they're ready. They trial-close me. They generally ask me one thing: how they can get started to earn the improved profits I've shown them by working with me. 'How do we get started?' they'll ask me. 'What do we have to do first?' Sometimes they'll come right out and say, 'When can we get this show on the road?' Up to that point, they're not ready."

"How do you know?" the manager asks.

"Because they're asking me other questions to make sure in their own minds that the improved profits I'm proposing to them can actually come about for them in their business. They're not refusing to buy. They're studying the implementation. Will it work the way I say? When they see it, they want it."

"So why can't you hurry it up by making them see it sooner? Test them once or twice: 'Do you see it yet? Do you want it now?' Instead of waiting for them to become as smart as you are, make them jump!"

"That's not what's happening," the salesperson says. "I'm the one who's waiting—waiting to become as smart as they are in taking what I sell them and integrating it into their operations. That's what they're telling me all this time. 'We have this problem here; how can we solve it? Here's something unusual about our operation; how can we get around it?' I'm learning all the ins and outs of their business so that when they buy, they get what I've proposed to them."

"Well, let's go up now," the manager says. "Someday when we have more time you'll have to help me learn how to let the other guy close me."

"I just did," says the young man.

Whenever You Want to Go Home Early, Start Talking to the Customer About Your Business Instead of His

"Your manager complains that you talk too much," the general sales manager (GSM) says to the representative. "Is there any truth to that?"

"He told me the same thing," the representative replies. "He told me there was a rule in selling that was older than both of us: When you've made the sale, stop talking and get out. He said I violated that almost all the time."

In vendor selling, where commodity products are being sold on the basis of their price, and where other considerations rarely apply, knowing when to stop selling—that is, knowing when to stop justifying price—may still be the best strategy. Vendor selling is similar to hypnosis. The sales representative focusses the customer's attention on a narrow range of sales points *and the price*. Any extraneous information is to be avoided. Objections are to be overcome, "Yes—butted" to death. Trial closes are to be slipped in at every opportunity. If the representative keeps on talking, an opening will surely be created among the trial closes.

None of these things apply to key account sales. Here, the situation is almost exactly the opposite. When the key account customer buys, that can be the time to start, not stop, selling.

"Why do you talk so much?" the GSM persists.

"Well," the representative says, "I read somewhere that the best customer is someone who is already a customer. Especially if he's a key account, since he's already established himself as someone who needs what you have to sell him. If you can help him discover additional needs that you can serve, he ought to be receptive to buying even more. So once he buys, I figure he's my best customer. That's why I go on selling him."

"But what about what you just sold him?" asks the GSM. "Aren't you afraid you'll endanger that?"

"I'm always careful to wrap things up on a step-by-step basis before I go on," the representative says. "But then I try to link what we've just agreed on to a new need that I can fill. Some salespeople sell one sausage at a time. I sell links."

Vendor salespeople are trained to sell sausages. They react to a request for a proposal, submit a bid that concentrates on meeting its specifications, and hope to come away with the order. Key account selling is largely *initiative* selling, however. There may be no request for a proposal, just a need that a sales representative and his customer both perceive. Instead of just going after an order, the representative goes after the customer. He tries to come away with an improvement in the customer's business that he has helped to create. He also brings back with him information on the next problem he can solve or the next opportunity he can help his customer achieve.

"How do you know what to talk about?" the GSM asks the representative. "After all, the more you talk, the greater the risk of making yourself sound like a fool. Instead of making two sales, you can lose everything and walk home empty-handed."

"The difference between sounding like a fool and making sense to a customer is to know the customer's needs and direct the conversation to them," says the representative. "Its all in the precall, as I like to say. Once I know what I'm going in to sell, I study all around it. What other problems are connected to this one? If we solve it, what is the next situation that the customer will turn to for improvement? Maybe I can kill two birds with one stone and make a more comprehensive sale—a bigger unit at a larger price. Maybe the problem the customer perceives is really part of a larger one or the logical *second* step in a problem instead of the first step. Those are the kinds of things I study."

"So what you're saying," the GSM sums up, "is that, as long as you confine yourself to talking about the customer's problems, you're on safe ground."

The ground is more than safe that way. It is veined with gold. There is no talk that is more profitable for a sales representative than the dialogue with customers about their problems. Once a customer has indicated that he has faith in a supplier and entrusts the solution of one important problem to him, he is ready to entrust another. The representative's role is to be the catalyst. He must come prepared to talk business: the *customer's* business. He must suggest problems to explore, contribute his own knowledge of their effect on the customer's business, and earn the cooperation of the customer in pinning them down so that he can propose a solution.

"The reason you talk so much, then," the GSM says, "is to get the customer to talk to you about more of his problems once he has become certain that you can solve at least one of them for him? Is that the story in a nutshell?"

"That's the key," the representative agrees. "Always talk customer; talk about his needs; and keep talking as much as you can."

"Let me ask you something," the GSM says. "If you and your customers talk so much, how do you ever complete a sales call?"

"Whenever I've learned enough, I just start talking about my own product. Then the customer says I talk too much, and we both get up and go home."

Objections Are Not Things to Be Overcome—They're to Be Provoked

The sales manager focusses his gaze on the back of the room and zeroes in on one of his representatives. "How do you handle it?" he wants to know. "It's one of the most important professional selling skills. How do you overcome objections?"

"I don't," the representative answers.

"You don't?" the manager asks skeptically. "What do you do with them?"

"I encourage them."

"But there's no way you can sell in the presence of objections," the manager retorts.

"There's no way I can sell in their absence," is the representative's reply.

Like the opener and the trial close, overcoming the customer's objections has become an article of faith in selling. Sales representatives are taught timeless strategies to counteract a protest—or even a silent stall—that gets in the way of their sales strategy. They are taught to say, "Yes, but . . ." allowing them to overcome agreeably. Or they are told to say, "That's very interesting" even when it isn't, or "I'd like to get back to that a little later" even when they won't.

Then there are the "facts," those laundry lists of features and benefits presented as questions to allow the customer to save face by appearing to have known them all along: "Of course, you know that our product outperforms, outlasts, outsaves . . . ." Sometimes these traditional tools of the trade actually overcome an objection. Much of the time, a sale is made in spite of them, not as their result. But to *encourage* objections?

"Tell me, tell the whole group," the manager says, "exactly why you encourage objections. Don't we all get enough of them anyway?"

"Not the right kind," says the representative, "not the kind that

126

can teach me what I need to know about the customer's business. Those are the ones I have to encourage."

"What kind are those likely to be?"

"The kind where the customer says to me, 'No, that's not right; that's not an accurate estimate of what it's costing me to perform this function in my business.' Or 'No, that's too high a value you've placed on the alleged new profits I'd make by increasing my sales to this market while decreasing them to that market. Here, let's use this number as being more accurate.' "

"But what's he saying that in response to," the manager asks, "certainly not your product presentation or your price?"

"Oh, no. That's not what I provoke him with," says the representative. "I put down in front of him my best estimate of how much cost I'm going to save him when he buys from me; how I'm going to reduce his inventory cost, or his labor, or his transportation; whatever. Or I show him how much I can help him earn from new sales of his own product when he buys from me—added sales from existing customers or entirely new ones. By presenting him with my figures, I am saying, in effect, 'O.K., object to them. If you keep silent I'll make the inference that I'm right. Otherwise, tell me where I'm wrong by what you object to.' "

"And when he objects, what do you do then?" the manager asks.

"I ask him to tell me how much I'm off, and how come. What it is about his business that makes his answer what it is. That's how I learn his peculiarities. Sometimes I even challenge him. 'That doesn't jibe with my experience,' I'll say. That way, I object to his objection. I learn even more."

"When all the objecting is over, yours and his, what do you have left?"

"Something we both can agree on: a figure for his costs that I can then try to reduce, or a sales target that I can help him achieve. It's our whole basis for working together."

The manager strokes his chin. "I can see agreeing on the facts before you sell. But what do you do after you get agreement on what the customer's problem is? Aren't there more objections after that?"

"What is there to object to? Once we agree on the problem—or maybe it's an opportunity—we can work together to put into effect the best strategy to solve it. We go through a series of agreements:

what the products and services will be that he needs to buy from me, when he can expect to see the first signs of improvement, how we will measure them."

"You don't get any more objections after that?" the manager asks.

"Oh, if I do, they're nice ones: couldn't we have saved even more, couldn't we have made the new sales come in even faster? These are good objections because he's telling me he likes what I did but he could learn to like it even more."

"Well," says the manager. "I hope everyone at this meeting has benefited by this novel treatment of the handling of objections. Just bear in mind, however, that the discussion would never have taken place if I had not applied one of my favorite selling strategies: deliberately provoking objections."

If You Don't Get Involved in the Customer's Problem, You Probably Won't Be Involved in His Solution

"What is your definition of a sales representative for this company?" the manager asks one of his average performers who is sitting across from him.

"A problem solver," the representative replies.

"And what is your test of how well you live up to that definition?"

"The number of problems I solve—successfully."

"And," the manager persists, "how can you tell in advance—before you actually make the sale—that you're carrying out your role properly, that you're on the right path to a successful solution?"

The representative draws a blank.

Some managers use a simple, yet virtually foolproof, method of qualifying their representatives as problem solvers: They analyze their proposals. These managers systematically time their salespeople, not only the total time of their proposals but how much time they focus on the customer's problem, and particularly *how long they can go without falling back on discussing their own product*.

"How far into a proposal do you think a professional problem solver ought to be able to go before mentioning his product for the first time?" the manager asks.

"For the first time? Maybe one third of the way at best, one quarter more likely," the representative says.

"Two thirds," the manager says firmly, "three quarters is even better if he or she wants to solve problems for customers of this company."

The representative stares at him. "How can you go that far? What is there to talk about the rest of the time?"

Customers, being human, are obsessed with their own problems. They think about them all the time. Many problems are persistent. They resist solution, but eventually something can be done about them. An even greater number of problems, however, can be solved only partially or temporarily so that a few of their symptoms are alleviated. Customers live with stubborn problems, piecemeal remedies, and costly but ineffective solutions. You might think they would have enough of them without having suppliers come in and talk about them some more. But until a problem is solved, a customer can never hear enough about it.

"I want you to take advantage of all those partially solved problems out there," the manager says. "I want you to focus every proposal you make on the same subject your customers focus on. I want you to lock in on a problem from beginning to end. What are the most important aspects of a customer problem you should dwell on?"

"Well, I'd start with how severe it is," the representative answers, "then get into the other basics: how long it has been going on, what its causes are as we see them, what the various parts of the problem are—the ones we can solve and the ones we can't. Oh, yes. I would also bring up the problems caused by the problem; how it affects specific parts of the customer's business."

"Give me an example," the manager says.

"Take a problem in a single function of a customer's business, such as production. What's affected? Maybe production scheduling; the product doesn't get out or it gets out unevenly. This raises hob with costs like labor, energy, materials storage—the whole works. How's that?"

"What about a problem that spreads to more than its original function?" the manager asks.

"Then take forecasting. A problem there makes the costs of administering the function rise. The same problem, whatever it is, can affect inventory control. A problem there can affect warehousing, distribution, sales. At each step of the way, new costs are added on."

"Does that give you enough to go on?" the manager continues. "Is there enough meat there, do you suppose, to keep you involved with the problem for a while?"

"Yes."

"Then what will you move on to?"

"Our solution?" the representative asks.

"So, it's still not product time? Good," says the manager. "How long do you think you can stay on the solution?"

"That is what we're really selling, isn't it? I guess I should hit it as hard as I can, spell it out in detail in terms of how it affects the problem. I'd mention all the components of the solution. Say, isn't here where I could make my first mention of our product?"

"I suppose so," the manager says, smiling. "If you're all that impatient. And how would you regard your inclusion of the product at that point? Would it be the climax of your proposal?"

"Just another part of the solution, actually. An important component but no more than that. Anticlimax is probably a better word."

"Now," says the manager, "you're seeing our product the way our customers have always seen it. Maybe they'll have a chance to see us in a new way too."

Who Wins in the Jungle Out There: Lead Elephants or Jet-Propelled Butterflies?

How does a customer sense that we really know his business: by the thickness of our proposals or by their thinness?

Field sales manager: I'm telling you this now so you'll be prepared when it happens: At our next sales meeting, I'm presenting you with the Lead Elephant Award.

Sales representative: What for?

Manager: I give it annually to the salesperson who consistently puts together the heaviest proposals. If you win it twice, you retire the trophy, and we retire you.

Representative: That's not fair. You can't judge proposals by weighing them.

Manager: No, but that's what you seem to be asking your customers to do. Why do you use so much paper—do you have stock in a pulp mill?

Representative: It takes paper to sell. The whole point is to get their attention and keep it.

Manager: I'm surprised your customers don't get pneumonia from the breeze of all those pages turning. What do you think the purpose of a written proposal is?

Representative: To tell customers all about our products and why they should buy from us.

Manager: I disagree. As I see it, the purpose of a proposal is to tell the customer *something about himself,* preferably a specific problem that we can help solve.

Representative: Tell him about himself? He already knows that, doesn't he?

Manager: Not as we see it through our eyes, he doesn't. For him to see it our way, which is with what I call *solution eyes,* he'd have to be in our business.

Representative: You're saying that he sees his business with what, *problem eyes?*

Manager: That's a good way to put it. He sees his problems as they affect his business, just as if his were the only company in the world that ever had that particular problem. And as long as he thinks about it in that way, he'll never see a solution.

Representative: But our product's the solution, isn't it?

Manager: Never. Products, ours or anybody else's, don't solve anything. What does it take to bring about a solution to a customer's problem?

Representative: O.K., I know: recommending the right product in the first place. Then applying it, following through to control its performance, maybe teaching his people how to use it, and then upgrading it or replacing it later.

Manager: In two words, *adding value.*

Representative: Right. So the purpose of a proposal is to single out a customer problem, show him what it looks like with solution eyes, and add value with the solution.

Manager: I'll buy that as far as it goes. But there's more. It's not only the solution that must add value to the customer. The proposal must add value, too.

Representative: How can a presentation do that without winning a Lead Elephant?

Manager: Let's ask ourselves, What are the customer's values that a proposal is trying to add to?

Representative: Well, for one, I suppose the value he puts on his time. In that sense, we can add value by coming to the point quickly and staying there. Is that what you mean?

Manager: Yes. What other values can we add to?

Representative: His knowledge. We can help him learn how to run his business better by solving his problems. We can even help him head off problems before he has to allocate resources to deal with them. We can add value to his scarce resources, to his best people, his capital funds, his corporate image. There must be dozens of things.

Manager: There are. What's more, we must also try to add value in areas where we don't have any role to play at all. We must help give him the freedom to concentrate on how he wants to run his business, to exercise his management prerogative.

Representative: The more you say, the bigger the proposal becomes.

Manager: Quite the opposite. The smaller it becomes. Let's sketch it out right here. What's the first thing we have to say?

Representative: According to you, we have to start out by telling the customer about himself: here's something you can do to improve your business.

Manager: Good start. What's next?

Representative: Our solution-eyed view of the problem. What it looks like solved; what the added values would amount to, the way it will be after we apply ourselves to it. How's that?

Manager: Keep going. What follows?

Representative: We'd better tell him how we're going to get him from where he is to where we say he can be. We can take him inside the solution, show him how it will solve the problem, and prove that it's the best buy for the money.

Manager: Suppose you stopped right there. Have you "proposed" to him—proposed a solution to his problem and proposed that he accept our expertise to put the solution to work?

Representative: Yes. But what about all our product information. Where does that go?

Manager: Make it the tail of the kite, not the kite. Remember, that's *not* what customers buy.

Representative: So when competitors come in and make the customer familiar with all the ins and outs of their products, I shouldn't care?

Manager: Not if you're sure you've made the customer familiar with all the ins and outs of our solution to his problem.

Representative: And when competitors hand in 3-inch-thick proposals that seem to indicate they've devoted all their time to the customer's interests, I shouldn't care either?

Manager: Not if you're sure you've done your homework in a more dedicated manner so that you can boil down the customer's problem to its essence and specify exactly the right solution.

Representative: You're sure that if I do that I'll be all right?

Manager: Better than all right. You'll be the first winner of my new Jet-Propelled Butterfly Award for the lightest and swiftest proposal.

A Customer's Biggest Problem May Be a Supplier Who Doesn't Understand Him

When a customer's business changes, his problems also change. His suppliers must change along with them or risk becoming just another problem.

Field sales manager: You've been selling to those same people for a long time. Why the problem all of a sudden? Is it them or you?

Sales representative: It must be them. I'm not doing anything different.

Manager: What's different about them?

Representative: The honeymoon is over for their main line of business. Competition is underpricing them; in some cases, it's offering a more innovative product, too.

Manager: In the jargon of our trade, that's known as becoming a mature business and losing price advantage as a result. How are they reacting to their change of life?

Representative: The usual ways. Meeting price cuts, boosting discounts, running deals. Some panic and a lot of pain.

Manager: Sounds to me as if they're going to have to do some things a lot differently from now on. Dealing with suppliers may be one of them. Yet you said you weren't doing anything different in working with them. How come?

Representative: I'm selling them hard. But I always sell hard. I've got the bases covered. So what's there to do differently?

Manager: Gear in with their new objectives, for one thing. You can be sure they'll have them. From this point on, everything you sell them has got to help them further those new objectives.

Representative: What do you mean, new objectives? They still want to make money—more now, as a matter of fact.

Manager: That's right. But they won't be able to make it in the same ways anymore. You said so yourself. So their objectives will have to change in terms of how much more they need to make. And their strategies for making it will have to change, too. Do you know the answers?

Representative: Do I know? No. Can I guess? Maybe.

Manager: Guessing about a customer's objectives and strategies is only slightly more dangerous than Russian roulette. If you're wrong, it can be fatal. But let's play the game anyway. If you were the customer, what would you be doing to make more money?

Representative: First, I'd lessen the dependence I've had on my biggest division for sales and profits, which are going to be harder to come by now.

Manager: What meaning will that have to people like us, the suppliers?

Representative: We may sell those people less, for one thing. We may have to lower price, for another. We may even have to change the mix of what we've been selling them.

Manager: Like what, for instance?

Representative: If they're going to have trouble with sales, maybe we should sell them something to give their products a new edge, some competitive advantage that could help them hold up price.

Manager: Do we have anything like that? And if so, are you selling it to them?

Representative: Well, not yet. It hasn't been a part of my regular mix.

Manager: But the customer's mix isn't regular anymore. Ours can't be either when we sell to him. Let's go on. What else would you be doing differently if you were the customer?

Representative: Look for a new big winner, I guess—a new product or a new market that can give high profits.

Manager: Where would you look?

Representative: The company's newest division. It's the smallest, but it has new technology. I'd do everything I could to step up the timetable for getting the first commercial product out the door. The sooner the better if I want above-average price.

Manager: Can we help the customer do that?

Representative: Actually, we have an excellent off-the-shelf product that the people over there could use. And we can package it with some unusual application services and sell the combination to them as a system. They'd pay us a premium for it if it could get them into the market sooner.

Manager: What other objectives would you have if you were on their side of the fence?

Representative: Aren't the two I mentioned enough? Why do they need a third?

Manager: To be fail-safe. If one of the two objectives you mentioned should be wrong or fail, that's a 50% wipeout. With three objectives, the chances of two out of the three succeeding are much better.

Representative: How about something a bit more certain than the second idea, just to balance the odds? Like an increased penetration into an existing market for another of their mature businesses. Same product, novel promotion.

Manager: Meets the requirement for apparent low risk. But if they do that, do we have a role to play?

Representative: We can share market information with them in the case of one of their businesses I'm thinking of. We know a lot about it. We can help them do more research, even set up their distribution to meet customer needs.

Manager: All right, now you have three possible new objectives for these people. How would you implement them?

Representative: I'd set priorities. The first would be to get costs down and sales up in my suddenly mature business. Then get my new business into the market and, with my left hand, perform my market expansion act where I'm at relatively low risk.

Manager: That's good enough right now as a guess for them. But what should our priorities be so we can sell to them?

Representative: The first is to learn about *their* priorities, not just make assumptions. Maybe we can even help them. Next is to get our own priorities in line with theirs: get our selling packages together, calculate how many dollars each one can contribute to the customer's objectives, and go tell them.

Manager: Would that be different from what you've been doing with this customer up to now?

Representative: I suppose I've been putting our objectives first, not his. As a result, I've been selling him more of the same when he's needed a whole new approach. He's been calling for help, and I've been helping us, not him. That's why neither of us has been getting anywhere.

Manager: So do you still see the problem we've been having with him as the customer's?

Representative: Sure. He just had a supplier who didn't understand the problem, that's all.

If You Make Sales, You Have a Job. It's a Career if You Manufacture Profits

If you ask your people who sell what they do all day, be prepared for some unusual answers—especially from the good ones. They hardly ever see themselves as making sales.

Field sales manager: Have you ever had any manufacturing experience?

Sales representative: You mean, Have I sold manufactured products? Sure, that's what I've always done.

Manager: No, I mean, Have you ever been a manufacturer yourself? Have you ever made anything?

Representative: How could I? I've been in sales. How many salespeople have been manufacturers?

Manager: Unfortunately, all too few. But they're the ones I like to hire.

Representative: Do you think the only way you can sell a product is if you know everything about how it's made?

Manager: Not at all. As a matter of fact, that could be detrimental. There'd be too much product orientation. What I'm looking for is people who are experienced in setting up a small manufacturing plant inside a customer's business and producing a profit on it.

Representative: What kind of plant?

Manager: As I said, a small shop. Just a few people: the salesperson and some support staff who'd be, say, technical, service, and financial. That would be the labor pool.

Representative: What would they make?

Manager: They'd make profit for the customer. That would be their only product.

Representative: What would they use for their raw materials?

Manager: Customer needs; raw needs, really, of two kinds. One would be a need to have their costs reduced in certain key functions that the manufacturing team could affect. The other would be a need to have their sales revenues increased in ways that the team could supply.

Representative: How plentiful are those raw materials? How long could they keep the manufacturer in business?

Manager: Forever. Only if the customer goes out of business will the need supply ever dry up.

Representative: O.K., so the raw materials are there. What's the manufacturing process consist of?

Manager: It's a hammer-and-anvil process. The anvil is the knowledge base of the customer's cost and sales opportunities—our knowledge of his raw materials. The hammer we use is our own capabilities, our smarts, so to speak. We beat on the raw materials and transform them into a more finished product.

Representative: What's the name of the product?

Manager: It's called improved profit for the customer. Or, to use sales terminology, we add value to the customer's raw materials by beating on them with our capabilities—after first learning the principal facts of his business, of course.

Representative: You make it sound like manual labor.

Manager: It is. Totally handwork. And every project is a custom job. But it's also one of the most advanced technology processes around.

Representative: Where's the technical skill in flailing away at customer needs with your capabilities?

Manager: You have to do it cost-effectively, that's where. That's the technical know-how. If you don't have it, what you can end up with is an unmarketable product called loss for the customer instead of profit. If you get into making losses, you go out of business fast.

Representative: So what do you do with customer profit once you make it?

Manager: The same thing you do with any high-quality product. You sell it. After all, you have a captive market. The customer is right there with you, and so it's a classic case of on-site manufacture.

Representative: How do you price it?

Manager: According to its value. And that usually means we price high. Profit, you know, carries a high value to anyone in business. It's actually the supreme value since it can go directly down to a customer's bottom line in many cases.

Representative: So you're looking for people who can go into a customer's business, set up shop as a manufacturer of profit for him, make the profit using customer needs and your own capabilities, and then sell the profit to the customer at a high, value-based price?

Manager: I couldn't have summed it up better myself. What's your reaction?

Representative: Well, I get the message. But I don't know that the world needs one more euphemistic definition of the sales function. Why the emphasis on manufacturing?

Manager: Because I believe that's exactly where most people who sell suffer a breakdown in their self-concept. They see themselves as sellers of products that other people make. I want them to see themselves as makers of their own product: customer profit.

Representative: I can understand looking at it that way. But really, what difference does it make?

Manager: When a salesperson takes up the position of being a manufacturer of customer profit, he stops selling the product someone else made and begins to sell his own product. He goes into business for himself instead of just being someone else's distributor. He acts more like an executive, and he treats his customer like a business executive, too. That means he realizes that the customer is in business to earn profit, not to buy products. So this sales representative tends to sell the profit he makes for the customer. That becomes his "product."

Representative: What becomes of the real product?

Manager: Customer profit *is* the real product. It's the only thing that's real in any sales transaction. There's nothing more real than money in the bank. You can see it, touch it, spend it, or invest it. What could be more real than that?

Representative: Right. I should have said, what becomes of the physical product—what's a good word for it—intermediate product?

Manager: It becomes part of the hammer we use to pound out the customer's profit. It's a part of our capabilities to make an impact on our customer's needs. That gives it a proper place.

Representative: Why shouldn't the physical product be featured in a more prominent place, the way most salespeople do? You're the first person I've ever talked to who didn't make the product king.

Manager: If we had products that reigned supreme over competition, maybe we'd be tempted to go out and sell them. In our industry, like almost every industry I know, nobody's product stands tall enough to be king, even for a day. We all have products whose benefits are pretty much at parity with one another. So why push something that's so undifferentiated customers won't pay a higher price for it?

Representative: But how come a salesperson who manufactures customer profit doesn't manufacture profits that are the same as any competitor could make for the same customer? Isn't it the identical problem?

Manager: That's the whole point. It's not. It never is. No two profit manufacturers ever make the identical profit for the same customer. They don't have the same capabilities to work with. They don't have the same team. They don't have the same individual smarts. They don't always choose to work on the same customer needs at the same time.

Representative: What's to prevent a customer from doing business with several profit manufacturers at once?

Manager: Nothing. That's what a customer should be doing: working with as many so-called suppliers as possible to get them to provide added profits to his business. What we want to do is to stake out our particular area where we can bring something special to the party and become our customer's profit manufacturer in that area. That's why I need to hire makers of money: the key word is *makers,* people who beat out profit for our customers.

Representative: Suppose I'm interested in becoming one of your profit makers. Where do I apply?

Manager: I'll send you to see a couple of our major customers. Apply with them. Find out if they'll accept your manufacturing plant inside their business and if they'll give you access to their raw materials, their needs. They know our capabilities, but they don't know you. If they think you'll make money for them, they'll call and force me to hire you.

Representative: I never heard of customers hiring supplier's salespeople.

Manager: That's because you never heard of a supplier's salesperson who was really a manufacturer of the customer's profit.

If You Want to Be a Customer's Sole Supplier, Act as if You Already Are

It's easy to say to a customer that we want all of his business. But it's even better if we give him a preview of what it would be like.

Sales representative: The last manager I worked for believed that getting on the customer's list was everything. Make sure we're always considered, that was his motto. He figured we'd get our share that way. But your philosophy is totally different: Don't be content to be a second source. Be the sole source.

Field sales manager: If you can have it all to yourself, why settle for less?

Representative: But that's just it. How can you get it all to yourself? Everybody wants the security of alternative sources of supply . . . to say nothing of the price leverage that's generated by playing one off against the other.

Manager: Some customers do. But it's a mistake to believe that multiple sources are a basic need of human nature; otherwise, we'd all have two wives, two jobs, and everything else. How about considering the advantages to a customer of having us as a sole source—or at least the major supplier?

Representative: I'd like to, really I would. But every promise I can make to a customer, the other guy can make, too. So why buy exclusively from me?

Manager: Let's see whether there are any reasonable answers to that question—reasonable to the customer, that is. Start small. Why would any customer in his right mind want to deal with us on a nearly exclusive basis?

Representative: One obvious reason could be that he'd surely get to know us that way—he'd know our capabilities, our talent mix, our support services. We'd be predictable to him, almost like a part of his own business.

Manager: Would that be good or bad?

Representative: Good. And there's the other side of that coin, too. While he was getting to know us, we'd be getting to know him. We'd know the ups and downs of his business, his demand cycles and problem markets. Simply put, we'd know his needs today and his plans to meet his future needs.

Manager: Would that be good or bad?

Representative: Good. In fact, excellent. There's even more, though. Think of how close we'd get to his people, how well we'd know his buying preferences, the values he looks for in what he buys, and who influences him. And we'd know something automatically that right now takes us a lot of work and time even to approximate: the politics of his organization, which very often makes the real difference between our getting the business and losing it. And before you ask me whether that would be good or bad, it would be very, very good.

Manager: Think a little deeper with me about what you're saying. We'd get close to him, you're saying, as we've never been before. We'd have access. That's nice, but what we pay off on is sales, not just the ability to spend time with someone who can award them to us. How could we capitalize on our trustworthy position of having access?

Representative: By teaching everything we know about our products, and why he should buy from us.

Manager: No, no, no. If we did that, it would be goodbye access. Before we teach anything, what must we do first?

Representative: O.K. First we learn, right? We learn about the customer's needs, wants, problems—what he will accept as solutions for them. We learn these things so that we know them better than anyone else on the outside.

Manager: You remember all the sales-skills training you've had? What aspect of it applies to what we're talking about?

Representative: Asking questions. Listening to answers. Making ourselves easy to talk to.

Manager: Right. And it's just at this point that traditional selling skills break down because they don't tell us what kind of questions to ask, what kind of answers to listen for, and how to make ourselves not just easy to talk to but absolutely necessary.

Representative: How could we be necessary to a customer?

Manager: By the kinds of questions we ask, making sure we get at the chief problems that are bothering the customer. And by the kinds of solutions we can suggest to resolve those problems. What are the main areas you'd get into if you had the virtually unlimited access of a sole supplier?

Representative: The first thing I'd look for would be the problems that we're best able to solve for the customer, and that would make the greatest difference to him if we did solve them . . . pardon me, not *if* we did, *when* we did.

Manager: Thank you. And if we acted in this way, how would you describe the role we'd be playing with him?

Representative: We'd be the customer's problem solvers, wouldn't we? Actually, we'd be solving two kinds of problems for him. An operating problem of some kind. And a cost problem. We'd be his multiple problem solver. Is that the answer you want?

Manager: It's the answer the customer wants. Or at least it's one half of the answer. What's the other half?

Representative: Well, if one part is solving problems, the other half could be looking for new opportunities for the customer. That's an area where we could really swing with our technical support capabilities and our research. We could work with him on new products, new ingredients, new market developments—all kinds of new opportunities.

Manager: In this aspect of our work with the customer, how would you describe our role as he would see it?

Representative: It wouldn't be problem solving, so it must be problem avoiding. Better yet, let's put a positive cast on it. How about opportunity developing . . . I have it! How about sales development for the customer?

Manager: I'll buy that. How about reviewing what we've said? Be the customer's problem solver. Be the customer's sales developer. Be the customer's alter ego in the areas of his business where we could make a vital contribution. If we could be these things to key accounts what kind of alternate supplier do you think we'd be?

Representative: The most desirable kind imaginable. The kind that any customer would prefer to do business with, maybe even . . .

Manager: Be careful. You almost said the word *exclusively,* didn't you?

Representative: It just seemed the logical idea, especially from the customer's point of view. After all, why wouldn't a customer want to do almost all his business with a supplier who solved his problems and opened the door to new opportunities for him? Why do business with anybody else?

Manager: No reason I can think of. So if we agree that being a sole source is very desirable, how do we get to that point?

Representative: It's obvious from what we've said: Act as if we already are. If we do the sole supplier's job with a customer, he'll do the exclusive customer's job with us.

5
Selling Like a Consultant

Becoming Partners with Customers to Help Achieve Their Objectives

Steer Your Sales with a Profit Compass: It Has Four Points That Lead to Money

"I wish I were starting all over again," the old man of the sales force says. "If I knew then what I know now, I'd make manager in three years instead of ten and there wouldn't be a competitor who could stay in my territory. What I don't understand is why nobody ever clued me in."

"To what?" I ask him.

"To the utterly simple set of rules that governs the selling process. I have a hard time seeing why it was almost two decades before the day when all the pieces finally fell into place."

"When was that?" I say, not even sure what pieces he is talking about.

"At a performance evaluation for one of my young salesmen two or three weeks ago. He's a nice young guy, but he was getting himself hung up on the mystique of what he called 'professional salesmanship.' You know, when to listen and when to speak, whether to overcome an objection or use the 'Yes, but' approach and roll with it: the trappings and the trivia of selling. So I let him have it. 'You'll never make it big,' I said, 'unless you start putting first things first.' "

"What first things?" I ask. The suspense is becoming unbearable.

"That's what he asked me. After I told him, I wrote it out. Here, have a copy. I call it the 'Salesman's Profit Compass' because it has just four points."

> **Point 1: whom to sell to.** Heavy users are perhaps 20%, or less, of our total customer load, but they contribute up to 80% of our profitable sales volume. So you should spend 80% of your time with them. Know who our heavy users are. Know their needs. Know which decision makers authorize purchases

151

to meet those needs. Spend the majority of your calling time with those decision makers and their influencers.

Then, get to be their chief problem solver. Become a member of their team. Because they will always know more about certain aspects of their business than you can, become expert in the one area where they are almost certain to be weakest: *knowledge of their own heavy users.*

Make your heavy users your key accounts. Use the remaining time to grow additional heavy users. When you've developed so much heavy-user business you can't handle it, come to your manager for help. That's the kind of problem he enjoys solving.

"I start with the heavy users," the sales manager said, "because they are where our protifable sales volume begins. Not in here, but out there in the market. Once you learn that and stop romancing the product line, you can become market-oriented. That's the beginning of being a salesman."

Point 2: what to sell. Sell your heavy-user customers your big winners, the moneymakers in our line. Every time you match a big winner with a heavy-user customer, you're selling from strength.

Some of our leading products have been around for a long time. They're still winners, but competition now has its own knockoff models that offer similar benefits. You may feel so comfortable with the older items that you push them most of the time. Be careful. That can cost us dollars and cents.

Start phasing in our newer products. We still have certain preemptive benefits here, so we can fully brand these winners with a premium price. Do your homework on the newer brands so you can feel comfortable with them and teach your customers how to feel comfortable with them, too. Please don't use the excuse that you don't know our big winners because we don't tell you precise profit margins. We'll tell you what the winners are. You go out and sell them.

Point 3: how to sell. Heavy users buy our big winners for one reason: They help our customers improve their profit. It's as simple as that. Therefore, we have to use a profit-improvement selling approach.

This means that you must sell on the basis of how much of a customer's costs you can help him reduce, or how much new sales revenue you can help him obtain. These are the only two ways you can help him improve his profit. Either one is fine.

The two together are great. Profit improvement must become your major selling point.

To talk profit with your customers, you will have to know two things. One is how they make their profit. The other is how your big winners and your personal expertise can help them improve it. To learn how your customers make their profit, you must penetrate more deeply into their businesses than you may ever have done before. This is the best way that I can think of for you to spend your time.

"I call my men CPIs: Certified Profit Improvers," the sales manager says. "Once they discover that profit is the language their customers speak most fluently and become proficient in it themselves, they have the kind of dialogues that build new business. Then our salesmen don't have to worry about how to get a customer to talk or how to listen to him."

Point 4: who should do the selling. Just as we have big winners and dogs, our sales force has high producers and, well, semidogs. Our heavy-user customers not only deserve our high producers, they need them. These are the members of our sales force who know how to penetrate deeply into the needs of a heavy user. They put together solutions for them in the form of our major products and services, install these systems and make them work, and then sell the customer on upgrading and adding on.

Selling is a one-on-one game. When we have a high producer paired with a heavy user, we have the ideal situation. We can help the customer improve his profit because we have one of our best CPIs working with him. And we can improve our own profit because we'll be moving our big winners.

As our high producers begin to make this mutual profit improvement the crux of our sales efforts, they undergo a transformation. They become more like consultants to their customers than salesmen. Yet at the same time, they sell more profitably.

Another transformation also takes place. Our customers become more like clients in a true professional relationship. This further improves our own profit by reducing the cost of our selling time with them and helps us maintain our premium prices.

"You see what I mean about starting all over again?" the sales manager says. "With these four points, my 80-year-old Aunt Blanche in Kenosha could be a high producer."

Say All You Want— Nothing Happens Until the Customer Asks You "How?"

Selling has always been a give-and-take activity, a question-and-answer form of persuasion that has worked to the advantage of the salesman who could get the customer to ask the right question or avoid the wrong one. In the first fifty years of this century, salesmen were taught that their worst handicap was to be unknown. The toughest question they could be confronted with, then, was a "who" question from their customers, such as "Who did you say you were?" or its companion, "I don't know who your company is."

For half a century, salespeople hammered away to create high awareness for themselves, their companies, and their product lines. This was the era of a slowly increasing interest in corporate advertising, brand identity, and corporate imagery that would "get our name known" in the marketplace.

By the 1960s awareness of most of the major suppliers had plateaued at an acceptable level. All but a few of them became immune from being confronted with "who" questions. Customers then began to ask "what" questions. "Now that I know *who* you are," they were saying in effect, "*what* are the unique benefits—or, at least, the relevant ones—of your products?"

This ushered in a decade of benefit selling. Salesmen laboriously tried to learn the difference between product features and characteristics as opposed to their user benefit values, and they were told to sell the benefits because that is what the customer really buys. For many companies, this was an especially difficult conversion to make after fifty years of selling product awareness and pictures of the factory. It also set off, inadvertently to be sure, a three-step process that temporarily gave a new lease on life to image selling. It went like this:

1. Just as the practice of selling product characteristics invited stereotyped objections that often paralyzed sales ("glass breaks" or "paper tears"), selling user benefits invited endless debate on comparative product merits.
2. To eliminate the debate, or at least neutralize it, benefits became standardized among competitive products.
3. As a result of product parity, sellers again turned to making image distinctions about themselves instead of performance distinctions about their products.

Now, selling is undergoing another evolutionary change in its approach to the customer. It is deliberately provoking the question, How? This is the best question of all for a salesman to respond to. For one thing, "how" is a third-level question. It presupposes that the first- and second-level questions of "who" and "what" have already been satisfactorily answered or bypassed.

A second reason for favoring it is that it means a salesman is being given his chance to sell. Only by getting the answers can the user come to know the ways in which he can use the product's benefits. This enables the salesman to take on his ultimate role of value adder to his customer.

There is a third reason for courting a "how" question, too. It is almost always the question that precedes the most conclusive question of all: "How much?" Many of the "how" questions that salesmen are being taught to induce are quite primitive:

"How can we apply your product to our own situation, which is different from the examples in your case histories?" (In response, of course, the salesman can ask his own version: "How is it different?")

Or: "How would you propose to convince our engineers to put your product into a use-test?" But some salesmen are learning to lead off their presentations with a stimulus that can open up the most effective of "how" questions: "How can doing business with you get me savings in my costs and improvements in my profitability?"

The best way to generate this sales-opening question is for the salesman to structure his presentations in the form of a profit-improvement proposal. This type of proposal, called a PIP for short, leads off with a selling proposition that follows these models:

- For a proposal to a steel company by a salesman for a refractory brick supplier: "This offers a way to lower your cost of melting a ton of steel by 15%, thereby improving your furnace's pass-along contribution to profit by a minimum of 5%."
- For a proposal to a chemicals processing company by a salesman for a glass-pipe supplier: "This offers a way to lower the cost of maintaining and repairing your fluid transport system by 25%, thereby improving the system's pass-along contribution to profit by a minimum of 10%."

The logical response to a profit-improvement lead-in of this sort is the question, How? The answer is the salesman's story. It will probably be composed of three parts: (1) the combined benefits of his product line, his company's application services, and his own personal expertise that make the profit promise plausible; (2) documentary proof from test cases or actual customer experience to validate his claims; and (3) a detailed order schedule that will allow him to implement his profit-improvement proposal by means of the necessary hardware and software from his company.

Proposing to lower key costs and improve customer profit is becoming the salesman's best working tool in a wide range of industries from food processing to high technology. In the coming years, it will take many companies far beyond benefit selling into "profit selling," which some sales managers call the best benefit of all. It will help put a lot of customer relationships on a quantified business basis and induce more rational purchase decisions.

It will also help end the kind of exasperating impasse that many salesmen now face. The glass-pipe salesman's story is typical. His customer, a chemicals processing engineer, will neither try nor buy glass pipe. Benefit selling produced only the response, "But glass breaks." Finally, in desperation, his sales manager counsels him this way:

"Next time you call, don't sell the product. Say only these words: 'I have a way to lower your cost of maintenance and repair by 25% by ending the problems of rust, corrosion, and contamination forever. This will help you improve your pass-along contribution to profit by a minimum of 10%.'"

The salesman asks, "After I've said that, then what?"

"Then leave," his manager says.

"But that's ridiculous," the salesman replies. "If I leave, he'll just get up and come after me, won't he?"

"Why should he do that?" the sales manager asks.

"Well," the salesman says, "won't he want to know how?"

Making Money Through Sales Is a Commendable Objective—Especially if You Start by Making Money for the Customer

"I just have one question for you," the general sales manager says to the recruit. "It's about your propeller, your power source. Would you mind telling me what you think that should be for a sales representative?"

"Sure," says the candidate. "Every salesperson should be powered by the desire to become a millionaire. That's the way I think about it anyway."

"You must have blown my district manager's mind when you told him that. Up to that point, he'd given you a 10 in every category we select for. That's why he wanted me to see you and discuss how we go about setting goals around here."

The manager gazes steadily at the candidate, liking what he sees, and then goes on. "I myself am fond of salespeople who are millionaires. As a matter of fact, I've never met a millionaire I didn't like. So I admire your objective, but I think you're confusing the end results with the means. I'd like you to think about it for a couple of days and then, if you're still interested in us, get back to me."

Manager, to himself: He's the kind of guy I want. A salesman who thinks in terms of money, not product; who realizes that dollars are the name of the game and not features, functions, and benefits; who can understand that products are transacted only because they can make money for both buyer and seller and that they ought to add value to everyone who touches them. But this candidate doesn't have his eye on the bull's-eye. He's still looking at the outer rings. I hope he'll think it through and come back.

Candidate, to himself: I really want to sell for this company. (as he goes down in the elevator): But what did that guy mean about confusing the end with the means? If I set the goal for myself to become a millionaire, that should automatically make my company rich too; if I make the commissions, they have to make the earnings. But maybe I put the cart before the horse just now. Maybe I should talk in terms of what I want to do for him and then tell him what I want the effect to be on me. That's it: straight benefit selling.

A week later, when the two are sitting across from each other again, the manager repeats his question: "If you come here to work, what power source will direct your efforts on our behalf?"

"The last time we talked, I said that I was powered by the desire to make myself a millionaire. Now I realize what I should have said. I'm going to power myself by the commitment to make my company more of a millionaire, to make my managers, especially the people I report to, all millionaires. In this case, that would include you in a place of prominence."

"Well," says the manager, "I can't find anything I wouldn't like about me becoming a millionaire. So, once again, I'm full of admiration for your objective, but I still think you're confusing the ends with the means. I'd like to ask you to think about it for a couple of days one more time and get back to me as quickly as you can."

Candidate, to himself (as he departs): What does this man want from me! First, I tell him I want my proof of achievement to be that I'm rich. Then I tell him he'd be rich too if I am and that the company would be making lots of money along with the pair of us. What more can he be driving at when he asks me to think it through some more?

After a few days the candidate realizes that he is going around in circles. Time is fleeting, so he takes a drastic step: He calls on some customers of the company he hopes to sell for. At a couple of them, he asks to talk with managers of the product lines that he would be selling into. At the others, he meets with the managers of the engineering and manufacturing operations who incorporate such products into their own.

With each of them, he asks just one question: "If you could choose any imaginable kind of supplier representative to work with, what would your ideal requirement be?" A few of the customer people think he is playing games with them or that he has entered a contest, especially when he gives them answers to choose from: (1) a sales representative who wants to be a millionaire, or (2) one who wants to make his manager a millionaire.

When he finally sits down before the sales manager for the third time, he doesn't wait for the manager to open the meeting. "I've found my true propeller," he says right off the bat. "I came back to tell you what it is—what it must be. If you think I'm wrong this time, then I won't be able to go to work for you because you will be wrong and I will be right."

The manager's raised eyebrows invite him to go on. "I want to make my *customers* into millionaires. That is my power source, my means, as you call it. If I propel myself with that goal in mind, then the results will be what I originally said would motivate me. I will become a millionaire, too, and so will you. But those are the ends, not the means."

The manager is nodding slowly. Then, abruptly, he looks at his watch. "We have a lot of customers who are always telling me how poor they are. How soon can you start making them rich enough to do more business with us?"

Don't Ever Ask How Much You'll Get Paid—Figure Out How Much It Will Pay for Them to Hire You

The sales manager looks the candidate over through squinted eyes and likes what he sees: big ears for listening, high forehead for thinking, clear eyes for seeing the point. "You'd be selling for me right now," he says, "but I don't have a spot for you."

"With all due respect," the candidate says, "you do have a place for me. That's why I've come here."

"If I do, it's news to me," says the manager. "What do you know that I don't?"

"I know one thing: Somewhere in your line there is a worst product. Either it isn't selling at all and everything else is carrying it, or it costs so much to sell that even when you move it you can't make a profit on it. But you can't drop it because the plant needs it to allocate its costs against. That's the job you have for me: to sell your worst product so that instead of acting as a drain on your profits it becomes another profit contributor."

The manager thinks about his worst product. Sure, he has one. It isn't a bad product, either. It doesn't have performance superiority, but neither do a lot of other products in the line. The worst you could say about it is that it is less than the best but no worse than its competition. Yet, no matter what he tries to do with it, nothing seems to work. Added features haven't done much; they just added to the cost. Lower price hasn't helped either; that lowered the margins.

He looks harder at the candidate. "How can you walk in here off the street and tell me you are going to do something that none of us have ever been able to do? Suppose I gave you my worst product. How would you sell it?"

"By not selling it," the candidate answers.

161

"I seem to be having a hearing problem," the manager says, "or maybe it's a failure in my understanding. But the next sentence you say will determine whether you continue to sit in that chair and talk your way into a job or whether you find yourself back on the street."

The candidate stays cool. He isn't shooting from the hip. He has been in situations before where, no matter what you did with a product, you still couldn't move it at a profit as long as you tried to sell the product. The customer was telling you something, but you weren't listening.

In effect, the customer was saying, "I don't want the product. I already have a choice of several products just like it—better, in fact, in some cases. I can get a higher-performing product and I can get a cheaper product. I can get a product that is both higher-performing and cheaper. What do I need yours for?" What he had been telling the customer didn't provide a good enough answer.

The answer, the candidate discovered, was never found in the product. Yet that was usually the only thing put in front of the customer: product features, product functions, product benefits, and product price.

"You've already proved that you can't sell the product on its merits as a product," he tells the sales manager, "so there's no sense in proving the same thing one more time. I'd like to prove something else: the merit of the *improved profits* that the product can contribute to your customers. That is what I'd like to sell, the profit values of the product and not the value of the product itself."

"How would you go about determining the product values of the product?" asks the manager. "Don't they come right out of the performance values that we build into it?"

"Not entirely," the candidate says. "They come mostly from the values the customer gets when he puts the product to work in his business or in his own products. That's partially dependent on our performance values, of course. But it is mostly due to the skill with which the customer puts the performance values to work. The more skill he employs, the greater contribution to the profits he can earn. Conversely, even the best product won't deliver its full capability if he doesn't put it to work with the maximum skill."

"I think I'm beginning to get the idea," says the manager. "You want to take my worst product and sell it by not selling it. Instead, you want to sell the product's ability to improve a customer's profits. Why do you feel that's a better offer?"

"Because the customer is telling you that he doesn't want your product. But no customer will every say he doesn't want his profit improved."

"If I said to you, 'O.K., you're hired; start selling our worst product,' what's the first thing you would do?"

"The first thing I'd do is *not* start selling the product," says the candidate. "Instead, I'd learn everything I could about how the product can improve a customer's profits. This would include how it can reduce a customer's costs and contribute to his profits that way, and how it can increase a customer's sales and contribute to his profits through higher revenues. Then I'd take a customer and work out with him how much specific profit I could add to his business. That is what I'd sell him."

"What about the product? What would you say about it?"

"I would describe its role in contributing to the profits I was going to improve for him, nothing else."

"How many customers do you think would buy from you this way?" the manager wants to know.

"If we got one more than is buying now, we'd already be ahead of the game, wouldn't we? And if two bought, we'd be doubly ahead. Everyone who buys means money in the bank that you are not getting now. If you can take a few minutes to calculate the costs you would allocate against me, we can find out very quickly how many customers I'd have to bring in to improve your own profits. Once you've paid for me, virtually every extra dollar I bring in will be clear profit."

"We've tried everything else," the manager says, "everything except selling the product by not selling the product. What kind of selling is this anyway?"

"It's not *selling*."

"It's *not* selling?" the manager asks impatiently. "First, the product isn't the product anymore; the product is profits. Now selling isn't selling. What is it then?"

"It's consulting," he says.

"Consulting!" the manager exclaims. "So *that's* what you've been doing with me. You didn't ask me for a job; you asked me for my worst product. You didn't ask me how much you'd get paid; you offered to figure out with me how much money you'd make for me. You didn't tell me how great a salesman you are; you sold me without selling. You are your own product, and you sold the product without selling the product, just as you said. I have just one more question for you. As sales candidates go, are you one of the best or one of the worst?"

"It doesn't matter," replies the candidate. "That's not what I'm selling."

The Product Doesn't Know How to Do Anything but Work—So You'd Better Know How to Do the Rest

"Go ahead," says the man who apparently is in charge of the customer's buying committee. "You might as well start your razzle-dazzle with us and get it over with. Why is your product the world's finest, fastest, most economical, most advanced—the most mostest we could buy?"

"It isn't," the sales representative says.

"It isn't what?" the customer asks.

"It isn't any of those things."

"Well, then, what is it?"

"It's a good product," the representative says.

"We buy only the best here, I'm afraid. We buy the best, and we sell the best. Good just isn't good enough. But before you go, tell me one thing: what does *good* mean, anyway?"

The sales representative pauses for a second before he answers. "Good means it does what a product should do; it works."

If sales representatives could be completely honest, many of them would give the same answer to their customers. There is not much else for them to say. Most of them sell mature commodity products; they offer me-too features and benefits. Their products are not inferior, but they are not superior either.

On a competitive basis, they have nothing to say except that the product does the job it was designed to do. How can a sales representative sell on that basis without getting clobbered on price? Without at least proclaiming differentiation, whether or not it exists, conventional wisdom says that the salesperson might just as well stay home.

"But does it work *best?*" the customer asks.

"That all depends," the representative says.

"On what?" the customer wants to know. "It either does or it doesn't. What could it depend on?"

"On what you mean by working best."

"Are you new at selling?" the customer asks with a note of annoyance in his voice. He looks at the rest of the buying committee in exasperation. "How can you not know what working best means? It pertains to the product's performance benefits, its operating advantages, its output."

"No," the representative says.

"No, what?"

"No, it doesn't work best in those respects."

"Well," says the customer, "what respect does it work best in anyway if it doesn't work best in those? What other respects are there?"

"How it contributes to profit," the representative says.

"How can your product work best in contributing to profit if it doesn't work best in the way it works?"

"Because of what comes with it."

"Which is . . .?" the customer asks.

"Me."

For the first time, the customer begins to see why the salesperson has steadfastly refused to be drawn into a discussion on the product. There is nothing to discuss beyond what he has already said: The product works. Having said that, there is no point in saying more. The product isn't what he is selling, anyway. His real offering is something that the product merely plays a role in: making a contribution to customer profit. Now, if the customer can be persuaded to ask the right questions, the representative will tell him how.

"What do you have to do with it?" the customer wants to know. "You make the sale, you make sure of delivery, and maybe you come back once to see how it's going. Then we never see you again until you have something else to sell, right?"

"Wrong," the representative says. "When I say you get me, I mean you get me. First, I want to present a proposal to you. It shows how I can improve your profit, by how much, and when. Because my product works, I'm including it in my proposal. I'm also including a financial analysis I made of your operation, the service package that I've put together to surround the product, and a training program to show your people how to integrate my system into your process. I'm going to be the manager of the system. You'll see me for the next three months until you get the full profits I'm proposing."

The customer looks quickly at the proposal. "Where did you get those numbers on our costs?"

"Some from your people, some from my own analysis. Where I wasn't sure, I was conservative. The profits on the bottom line probably are understated."

"I don't understand one thing," the customer says. "If your product doesn't work best, how can you improve our profits?"

"Because it isn't the product that makes the profit. It's the entire system I've designed around the product, including myself. I'm the most important part of the system because I'm the one who makes it deliver the profits I'm proposing to you."

"But surely the product plays a part," the customer persists. "How can your contribution be more important than what the product does?"

"Because the product doesn't know how to do anything but work. I know something no product knows: how to make it work in your operations to improve your profits. That's why I wrote out my analysis of how your costs can be reduced. You can prove to yourself that I know how to put my product to work for you."

The customer is thoughtful for a few moments. Then he says, "I have an idea. Why don't I go out to one of your company's competitors and get the product that works best and hire you to make it improve my profits best?"

"If you accept my proposal," the representative says, "that's exactly what you will be doing—assuming you're persuaded that the best product is the one that helps improve your profits best."

The customer rolls his eyes to the ceiling. But at the same time, the representative notices that he is taking out his pen.

How Well You Sell May Depend on How Long You Can Keep from Selling

"Do you all know what this is?" the manager asks the sales force assembled before him.

Everyone knows: it's a stopwatch.

"That is the easy part," he continues. "Now for something harder. What do you think I'm going to do with it?"

No one responds, so he says, "I'm going to accompany each of you on your next key account call. We're going to go before a major decision maker—anybody but a purchasing agent. I'm going to listen to your presentation and I'm going to time you, not on how long you take but on how long you can go without once mentioning your product."

Almost all the salespeople squint quizzically at their manager, making sure he is serious. "But our product is what we'll be selling," one of them says, "How can we go for very long without mentioning it?"

Another asks, "Is this a new guessing game? Is there a prize for the customer who guesses first what we're selling?"

There is a method to the manager's seeming madness, however. His people's sales calls are becoming self-seeking and self-serving. They are almost totally "we"-oriented: We make the best product, we have the best reputation, we have the oldest established business, we have the most dependable delivery and the fairest prices.

At the purchasing-agent level, this is often acceptable enough. But every time a salesperson penetrates above that level to a middle management supervisor or higher, he finds himself being sent right back down again. The sad part of the matter is that none of the salespeople seem to care. Talk to them about selling at a higher entry point and all you get is a blank stare. They only want to know what it will do for them, and there is no way to tell them that. That is why the manager hit on the stopwatch idea.

On the first accompanied call, the salesman lasts less than three minutes before he falls back on his product. On the second, another member of the force traps herself in a competitive comparison and, insisting that "we are better," has to explain who "we" is. It takes almost the same length of time.

The longest holdout is a little more than five minutes. The salesman says nothing about the product all that time, but he says nothing else of importance either.

At their next meeting, the salespeople throw themselves on the mercy of the manager. "We're becoming tongue-tied," they say. "It has taken us years to get our product features and benefits down pat. We've got the best story to tell in the industry. Now we can't say it. The net effect is that we're working for the competition. What is more worthwhile to talk to a customer about than the product, especially when it is the best in its field?"

The manager gives them his answer: "Talk about what the customer wants most to hear."

"What's that?" the people want to know.

"You tell me," he replies.

"If I were a customer," one saleswoman says, "I'd want to know what suppliers were offering what products at what prices."

Another member stops her. "You wouldn't be a customer for long that way, if that was your priority. That's a salesperson's answer. A customer's answer would be that he'd want to hear ways of running his operation better so that he'd be a sharper competitor, grow his business faster, increase his market share, and take more money to the bank. That's what I'd most want to hear."

"But we're product salespeople, not customer consultants," a third persons says.

"And if we stay that way," the manager says, "we'll lose all our business to the consultants. They're the ones the customer want to hear from."

"So how do we consult?" everyone wants to know. "Give us the feature-and-benefit story for consulting."

The manager says, "There's only one benefit: The customer hears what he most wants to hear from you. There's only one feature: Know the customer's business and talk to him about how you can help him run it better."

"Are you telling us that if we talk to customers the way consultants do, we can do better as sellers than if we tell our product story?"

"Why not try it for yourself the next time you call?" the manager suggests. "Take your stopwatch out and time yourself. How long are you spending talking to the customer about bettering his business? How long can you go without your product being mentioned? And then the crucial question: How long will the customer talk to you?"

"Does that mean that a longer sales call is a more successful sales call?" they want to know.

"That depends on who's talking. If it's you, the answer is no. You're just taking a long time to sell, and you're probably "unselling" yourself along the way. But if it's the customer who's talking, he's doing one of two things. He's buying or he's giving you information on which to sell. Either way, it's your best chance for success."

"What's the most important thing to look for when the customer is doing the talking like that?" someone asks the manager.

"See how long he can go without mentioning your product."

One Advantage of Selling Systems Is That You May Never Have to Sell Again

Marketers ask themselves, "How can I sell like IBM?" By way of answer, most of them have assembled what may best be called pseudosystems. Some of these have been put together by combining sets of products whose operation seems to complement each other. Occasionally, a service is tacked onto a product, and the duo is christened a system. Insurance, maintenance, and repair are frequently used this way. Sometimes a sales manager will even confide, "We've always provided that service anyway, but now we call attention to it as part of a 'system'."

The greatest danger of marketing a pseudosystem is not risk of exposure, however. The problem is profiting from the combination sale. With luck, adding on a service will neither carve a significant piece out of profits nor inflate the system's price above what the market will pay.

True systems selling is a good deal more complex than the cheap imitation. Unlike its jerry-built namesakes, it generally works to both the customer's advantage and to the supplier's profit interests. As with many complex marketing strategies, systems selling is based on a relatively simple formula, which has five parts. Any company can practice it whether consumer, industrial, or service. Yet its application at the customer level requires sales force education and management of the most sophisticated type. For no matter how systems selling is sliced, the salesman is the key to making it work.

Now let's take a closer look at the five major components of a systems selling strategy, whether IBM's or anyone else's.

1. Segment your market. The first job in systems selling is to identify the actual and potential heavy customers for your systems. In any market, the 80-20 rule will generally prevail. This says that only about 20% of all customers are heavy users; yet they can contribute up to 80% of all profitable sales generated by their market. Not only do heavy users buy more, but they may also buy more often. If 20% of your customers are heavy users, you *own* the market.

Heavy buyers, therefore, are your target. Naturally, they are also the bull's-eye for the competition. How well you handle the next four parts of the systems selling strategy, especially the second part, will determine who hits the bull's-eye with the greatest impact.

2. Seek out heavy-user needs. Once the major customer market has been segmented, its needs must be determined. This is the kind of strategy that makes systems selling customer-oriented. Only by diligent seeking within the customer's business can the salesman learn the customer's processes, the key aspects of his business that make it tick. This is the systems salesman's most treasured knowledge resource. Without it, systems that are put together run a high risk of being more self-serving to the supplier than need-serving to the user.

Seeking out customer needs is only one half of the problem, however. The other half is translating these needs into the form of problems that you can solve in ways that will help cut a customer's cost or boost his profits. This isn't always easy. Many needs cannot be readily translated into problems that you can solve this way. Others cannot be solved profitably by you. Your task, therefore, is to zero in on the relatively small number of major heavy-customer problems that you can solve most profitably *for both of you*. The definition of these problems becomes your definition of your customer's businesses. The solutions you create become your customers' definition of your own business.

3. Sell solutions to problems. The next step is to stop selling products and start selling solutions to customer problems. Because problems are usually caused by several interacting factors, they can rarely be solved by a single product or service. At this point, the concept of selling "solution systems" becomes relevant. The broader the problem, the more comprehensive its solution system can be.

Actually, systems selling is the ultimate expression of benefit selling. It is based on the assumption that the final benefit to the customer is relief from oppressive costs or the achievement of improved profits—sometimes both. Therefore, it accepts the challenge to reach these objectives by constructing a minimal system of products, attendant services, and the salesman's personal expertise in applying them to his customer's business.

The salesman sits at the apex of the system. He is its manager. He applies the smallest number of hardware and software components to the solution of each problem that will get the job done. In this way, he helps minimize his customer's cost, contributes to optimizing the customer's return on investment in the system, and begins the sausage-link process of applying successive systems to solve successive problems over a long-term relationship.

A supplier's R&D expertise is a key ingredient in selling solutions. It is from the supplier's technical base that most solutions come. The more fertile an R&D operation is, the easier it will be to add the promise of technical capability to the spectrum of benefits that the system user can employ. R&D can never be a substitute for a true system, as it is sometimes asked to be. But no successful system can operate without an assured research base supplying it with new solutions.

4. Circle systems with services. Systems selling works two ways. It increases the salesman's involvement in his customer's business, and it increases the customer's dependence on the salesman and the source of supply he represents. It is vulnerable to acute customer dissatisfaction when the system doesn't work, so the salesman must dedicate himself to keeping his customer's systems operating. He can best safeguard himself against the "unselling" effects of systems down time or failure to achieve objectives by surrounding his systems with two types of professional services. One is a package of preventive maintenance, repair, and replacement services that can keep systems running and help them perform at their specified rate of productivity. The other is educational and informational, important because the heart of every successful system is its information center.

Such a center may be a computerized database containing knowledge of customer markets, processes, economics, and relevant legislative and competitive restraints. It may be a library of books, reports, and manuscripts. It may be a school, or a curriculum of educational services and media. Ideally, it will be all of these, which can be harnessed together to teach systems customers how to maximize the benefits from their systems.

Every systems seller is automatically an educator. No part of any system is more important than its educational components, for it is on these that customer satisfaction is eventually based, as well as on the increasing sophistication that leads to customer demand for even more complex systems. In this regard, educational services are the best business keepers and business builders a system seller can have.

5. Supply consultative support. A systems salesman must be taught how to be a consultative salesman—a supportive counsellor of his customers who can work cooperatively with them over long periods of time. His objective is to help them improve their ability to solve the kind of problems in which he is expert.

Supportive counselling helps a customer upgrade both his knowledge and his level of confidence in the salesman. Anything that achieves these two goals must lead to additional business for the salesman. Consultative selling is a world apart from product selling. It relies on a continuing process of negotiation between salesman and customer, not sporadic persuasion by the salesman on an "I win/ you lose" basis. It forces the salesman to become unusually knowledgeable about his customer's manufacturing and marketing processes and about how profits can be improved by affecting one of them or both.

Perhaps the simplest way to sum up the strategy of selling in a consultative manner is to quote a veteran systems salesman for whom the strategy is now second nature: "I haven't 'sold' a system in years. Yet my sales go up year after year. How do I do it? I get inside the business of my key accounts. I uncover their key problems. I prescribe solutions for them, using my company's systems and even, at times, components from other suppliers. I prove beforehand that my systems will save money or make money for my accounts. Then I work with the account to install the system and make it prove out. Every success I have sells my next system for me. I may never have to 'sell' again."

In any industry, suppliers who are first to find a way to convert from product selling to systems selling can get a major preemptive jump on their competitors. Systems relationships, once established, leave little room for alternative suppliers. The IBM story certainly demonstrates this fact. For this reason, suppliers of such things as packaging, environmental protection equipment, automobiles, foods, and advertising media are moving rapidly into systems selling.

Eventually, as with all competitive offerings, rival systems will become relatively standardized. Then the premium will fall where it belongs in any selling situation—on the salesman himself, his customer expertise and systems management abilities, and on his dedication to help solve problems rather than just sell products.

Instead of Selling Harder, How About Getting Customers to Buy "Profitabler"?

The results of a sales campaign often have less to do with what we are selling than with how we propose it to the customer.

Field sales manager: I need your help in thinking up a theme for our annual conference. It should be unique and relevant to our business.

Sales representative: If it's going to be relevant, how can it be unique? Our problems are the same this year as they were last year. They're just one year older, that's all.

Manager: All right. Let's say relevant but uniquely expressed, so we avoid the deadening effect of the familiar.

Representative: That's hard to do. Just about everything is familiar by now. Every theme is a variation of one kind or another on the three basic themes, anyway.

Manager: What themes do you mean?

Representative: One is "Sell Harder." Some companies say it just that way, flat out. My former company used a variation of the theme, "Let's Have a Sell of a Year." Then there's "Back to Basics"— another way of saying the same thing. The basics are always hard to sell.

Manager: What's another theme?

Representative: "Sell Smarter," sometimes called "Using Brain Instead of Brawn." Conferences built around this theme usually feature strategic plays to improve sales: market segmentation, decision-maker analysis, things like that. Hard sell offends a lot of people, so the smart sellers say they'd rather be shrewd than rude.

Manager: Makes sense. What's the third?

Representative: "Sell Higher," or, as it's usually expressed, "Sell

Up." Conferences like this are built on the assumption that the real decision makers are upstairs, and if you can get to them, you can make new sales.

Manager: Which of the three themes do you recommend? Do you have one in particular or should we combine all three into a composite called "Sell Harder/Smarter/Higher"?

Representative: The trouble with that is its lack of uniqueness. The whole sales force thinks it's doing all those things right now and they're not working any miracles.

Manager: But those concepts are all relevant to our situation. Everybody may be doing them, but nobody's doing them well enough. That's probably why they're not working. It might not hurt to think about all three.

Representative: Sounds like a return to basics—in fact, the return to end all returns.

Manager: So suppose we vary it a little? How about "The Cerebral Sell—Heads-Up Selling to Meet Competition Head-On"?

Representative: Completely ignores the heart. Why not "The Coronary Sell—Sell Heartier, Not Just Harder"?

Manager: I'll ignore that. Maybe the best way to approach the problem is to ask ourselves what we really want to accomplish at the conference. What would you say is the single most important guideline we can give the sales force this year?

Representative: We could do worse than tell them when not to sell—you know, avoid the sales that take so long, or are too complicated, or are so small that even if we make them we end up with little or no profit.

Manager: But that's negative. We can't confer on *not* selling. How about turning it around to a more positive approach?

Representative: "Sell Where It Makes Dollars and Sense"?

Manager: But that's entirely "we"-oriented. Shouldn't we be customer-oriented?

Representative: Good idea. Why not "Sell Where It Makes the Greatest Sense—Dollars and Cents—for the Customer"?

Manager: Let's keep going. Why is that a good idea?

Representative: Because the customer is the source of our income. You've drummed that into our heads for years. If we make the customer happy by helping him make his business more profitable, he'll make our business more profitable by giving us his most profitable business. One dollar washes the other.

Manager: So how does that guide us—by telling us to be profit improvers for our customers and they will be profit improvers for us? If so, how can we say it in theme talk?

Representative: How about, "Remember the Name of the Game: For Us and the Customer It's Exactly the Same—More Profits"?

Manager: It would never fit on a banner. Even if it did, we couldn't afford it. Can you make it shorter?

Representative: Well, what we're essentially talking about is a first-things-first approach to our selling. Make sure the customer benefits by ending up with an improved profit from what we sell him. That way, he'll want to buy more from us than from competition. And that way, we can charge a higher price since we're benefiting him more. That benefits our own profit. What would you call this: "The Profit Priority"? Or, "To Sell Profitably, Sell Profit *Ably*"?

Manager: We're getting closer to something unique and relevant. The problem now is the best way to say it.

Representative: Maybe there's no best way to say it. Maybe any way to say it is right as long as it gets said.

Manager: Philosophically, I might agree with you. But in realistic terms, we have to have something to put on the banner, the buttons, and the book covers. That's what I wanted your help for . . . to come up with something short and sweet, like "Sell Harder," but more relevant.

Representative: O.K., you seem to like the harder/smarter/higher style of presentation, don't you? So I'm going to suggest something along the same lines. It meets your criteria: It's unique and relevant. And it has one more thing going for it. It's memorable, maybe even unforgettable. Are you Ready? "Sell Profitabler."

Manager: "Profitabler." I like it. For a word in the comparative tense, it's superlative. You're absolutely right. Once they hear it, they'll never forget it.

Representative: It's merchandisable, too. We can have an award for the rep who sells "profitabler" the "profitablest." We're limited only by our imaginations.

Manager: Which I think have gone just about far enough, if I may say so. There's just one thing more I need from you. We're all set from our own point of view; I can see the banner now, in green with white block letters. But what about the way we present what we're doing to our customers? Our "Selling Profitabler" might seem to them, when they hear about it, to mean we're taking new profits out of their hides.

Representative: How about a companion program for them—a "Buy Profitabler" campaign to stress that when they buy from us, they're going to be improving their profit and not just spending money to acquire products, services, and the like. And because their profit improves, ours will, too.

Manager: Sure. Anything that enables them to see our business and their business in common is good for both of us. Now, is there anything else we have to attend to before we lock all this up?

Representative: One more thing.

Manager: What's that?

Representative: When we take it the next step to get marketing's approval, let's be sure we sell it smarter and harder as we sell higher.

When You Make Your Last Call Selling Price, Make It Your First Call Selling Value

One of the greatest cop-outs in selling is to say that a customer buys only on price. If we examine it more closely, we may find that he won't even do that.

Sales representative: I've had it with that company. I've made my last call on the people over there and that's that, forever. Either reassign me or reassign them.

Field sales manager: What's the problem?

Representative: Price. They'll buy only on price. And even when I made them a price offer they couldn't refuse, they still refused it.

Manager: Tell me about it.

Representative: I've been calling on them now for almost two years. Every call is the same story. "Yes, we like your company. Yes, we like your quality. Yes, you meet our specs. No, your price is too high."

Manager: How have you tried to get them to buy?

Representative: You name it. Benefit selling. Sales negotiation strategies. Breakfasts, lunches, and dinners. I even reverted to features selling out of desperation one day, but that didn't work either. I decided on my do-or-die approach.

Manager: That's the one that died?

Representative: That's the one. It seemed foolproof. I thought if my price was too high, I'd let the customer set his own. Maybe then he'd buy. But he didn't like his price any more than he liked mine.

Manager: How did you make the offer?

Representative: I reminded him that we'd been avoiding doing business for almost two years. It was costing both of our companies money and not doing either of us any good. Then I ran through the checklist: "You like our company, right? You like our quality and the way we meet specs, right? But you don't like our price." He was agreeing with me all the way. Then I reached into my bag and pointed my secret weapon at him.

Manager: A gun?

Representative: An order form, all filled out except for the number of units and the price. I said to him, "These are for you to write in: how many you want to order and the price you feel you want to pay. You'll notice I've already signed the order on behalf of my company, and it will become official as soon as you complete it and sign it, too."

Manager: And then you were going to come to me for approval, carrying your resume, I presume?

Representative: You would have approved it for the same reason I wrote it up. Once we got them to try us, we'd have a good customer for years. Whatever we lost on the first order would be easily made up. But it's all academic now. It didn't work.

Manager: Why not?

Representative: A couple of reasons. First, he was shocked. "Set my own price?" he asked me. "You mean I can write in any price I want—a penny, even?" Then when I told him yes, we got into the second problem. He became suspicious.

Manager: Of what?

Representative: "What are you trying to do?" he asked me, "palm off a bad run on me that you'd otherwise have to scrap?" "No way," I told him. "We do our quality control at the plant, not with the customer." "All right," he said, "then you want to clean out your inventory of this particular model before coming out with a replacement; is that it? This is your idea of a closeout sale?" "It's no sale," I told him. Then he made his final guess. "You're going out of business," he said.

Manager: If we had more customers like that, he'd be right. So what happened?

Representative: He pushed the order form back across his desk at me and he said that something was going on here, and even though he couldn't figure it out, he wasn't buying it. And he didn't.

Manager: What do you conclude from all this?

Representative: If someone won't buy when he can set his own price, then price isn't the reason he won't buy.

Manager: But you said it was. Your exact phrase was, "They'll buy only on price." Since they won't even do that, why won't they buy?

Representative: I don't know. That's why I don't want to go back there ever again.

Manager: Suppose you were to take one more crack at them before throwing in the towel—one final fling where you could do anything. How would you sell?

Representative: I thought that's what I already did. What would I do now? Maybe I'd reverse the act. I'd go in this time and I'd say, "We've made some changes in everything but our quality. We've always been the best in the industry. That still holds. Now we've moved up our prices in keeping with our value. Let's say we're a third higher. But that won't hurt you, because I'm going to work with you to help you cut your process cost by an even greater amount than you pay me. So what you're paying out is a temporary down payment on a permanently reduced cost in a major process."

Manager: Suppose he said, "Show me."

Representative: I could show him. Even if I charged him 50% more, he'd still be coining more money than he'd be paying me, both in processing-time savings and labor costs. I should charge him 100% more. I could justify that, too.

Manager: It's a shame you've made your last call.

Representative: That really was my last call—as a price seller, that is. Now I'm going to make my first call as a value seller.

If You're Going to Be Best Salesman of the Year, Surprise Your Boss and Be It for the Customer

Some people who sell are convinced that they sell for the people who pay them. They're right—if they mean the customer.

District sales manager: I'd like a straight answer, Linda: Have you been moonlighting for the past several months?

Sales representative: No. Why?

Manager: I had a call the other day from the people at one of your largest accounts. The message they left was to tell me that the woman on their account had just won *their* annual award as Best Salesman of the Year. Before I got back to them I thought I'd ask you what it's all about.

Representative: It's true. They gave me the award. I won't be able to use the prize, though, until my vacation: It's an all-expense-paid two-week vacation to Hawaii for me and my "wife."

Manager: Your wife? What's a nice girl like you doing with a wife?

Representative: Nothing. But that's the way the award is worded. They're just a nice old sexist company that hasn't caught up with the real world.

Manager: I haven't caught up with how you can be the best salesman—or even the best salesperson—in a company you're not working for.

Representative: O.K., I'll tell you the story. It all starts with your teaching, so you're really responsible. Remember how you've pounded into us how we ought to hold quarterly review meetings with our key accounts to make sure they always know what we're contributing to them?

Manager: Sure. And not just to remind them of what we've

183

sold them, but to stress the financial advantages they've enjoyed from doing business with us.

Representative: Well, last December I had my fourth-quarter meeting with these people. I also used the occasion to make it my year-end review because I thought I had a really important story to tell.

Manager: What was it?

Representative: The installations I managed for them last year will add over $3.5 million to their bottom line. They'll get another $1.5 million from continuing cost savings flowing to their bottom line this year.

Manager: Nice. So you told them that?

Representative: Yes, but in much more detail. I took them through what we had done on a project-by-project basis. I showed them what their investment cost and how much return they receive on it per project. Then I took them through the year on a quarterly basis. I showed them their quarterly cash flow that I had worked out with their financial people. Since it was their own financial people, they couldn't argue with the numbers.

Manager: What did they say? "$3.5 million is a lot of money, and you must have been a super salesman to sell us enough of your products to make this kind of money for us. Thus you are the Salesman of the Year"—was that it?

Representative: None of the above. If they thought of me as someone who came in and sold them something all the time, I'd be spending my time sitting in their reception room with the rest of the vendors.

Manager: How do they think of you?

Representative: As the award says: as *their* best salesperson. Not yours, not ours, but *theirs.*

Manager: Now we're back to Go. If you're not working for them on the side, how can you be their best anything?

Representative: I was starting to tell you. I gave them the $3.5 million sweetener, but I asked them not to credit me with it since it won't actually be brought in until this year. I wanted them to know about it, you understand. But I didn't need it for what I wanted to accomplish.

Manager: Which was?

Representative: To prove my value to them as our account

representative in dollar terms that they can identify with their own business. That's why I took the next step. I reminded them that the $3.5 million was net profit—money they could take to the bank. Then I asked them the crunch question: How many of your own salesmen, I asked, have contributed an equal amount of profit to you based on their annual sales volume for the same year?

Manager: How many did they say?

Representative: Well, first they didn't know. All their records are in volume terms—so many units, so many gross sales dollars. But the question intrigued them. So they took a look at their major lines, calculated the profit on sales from their key products, and when they were finished all I saw was a roomful of raised eyebrows.

Manager: A lot of their salesmen contributed more?

Representative: None. In terms of who brought in the most profits to them, I did. They made more money on what I sold them than they made on what any of their own salesmen sold for the whole year!

Manager: So it's as if you were selling *for* them instead of selling *to* them?

Representative: Exactly. That's when I said to them, half jokingly, that I was their best salesman last year.

Manager: They didn't even have to pay you.

Representative: They looked at me very seriously for a few minutes, I guess to let the facts sink in. Then I did the awful thing that you heard about. I said, Haven't you had a contest all last year for the best salesman? Well, on the basis of profits, shouldn't I get it?

Manager: I'll say this for you: You have nerve.

Representative: No, they are the ones who have the nerve. They said, "I guess that's right, Linda. I guess you're our Best Salesman of the Year. You and your wife get the all-expense-paid trip to Hawaii."

Manager: So have they offered you a job?

Representative: Sure. And I took it. You want to know what it is? Oh, it's not to become an employee of theirs. I'm too valuable to them here. No, my new job is to teach our other accounts reps who call on the rest of their company how to become their Best Salesmen of the Year too.

Manager: And what will the effect of that be?

Representative: You'll be able to become their Best Sales Manager of the Year.

If Marrying Your Objectives to the Customer's Is Good Sales Strategy, Bigamy May Be Even Better

Commitment to doing a good job for the customer is one thing. Commitment to making sure the job you do improves customer profits is something else. The first without the second isn't anything at all.

Sales representative: We have a good product, don't we? Our price is fair and so are our terms. So why do I have to marry the customer to get him to buy?

Field sales manager: I've always said we have to learn to live with our customers, but that's not marrying them.

Representative: You keep talking about forming partnerships with them, becoming a member of their team, spending time in their home offices and plants, living their businesses with them. If that isn't marriage, I don't know what is.

Manager: What you've just said sounds like good selling strategy to me. What's your objection?

Representative: Who needs all that? They're not married to us. They tell us right to our face that we're an alternative supplier. Why can't I deal with them on the same basis—as an alternative customer? Why should I make a one-sided commitment to their businesses when they have no such commitment to mine?

Manager: The reason they've not committed is because you're not. The reason you're only a second source to them is because they're a second-, third-, or maybe even fourth-level consideration for you. If you really were married to them instead of just carrying on a dating relationship, both of you would be placing higher value on your relationship.

186

Representative: Why do you think marriage solves everything in a business relationship? It certainly doesn't personally.

Manager: Whether you call it marriage or living together, the advantages to you are the same. Only when you live together as partners can you really get to know each other. For you, that means getting to know your partner's business in an intimate way. There's no substitute for that kind of inside knowledge.

Representative: What can I learn as a partner that I can't learn as an alternative supplier, with a lot less investment in time and effort?

Manager: My way of answering that is in terms of what I call the three vital processes. The first one is the customer's decision-making process. From the outside, it always looks easy: Identify key executives by title and trace their lines of authority on the organization chart. On the inside, though, you can see how complex it usually is. Only partners get to learn the hidden agenda in a customer's decision making: who actually decides and who merely decides to decide. Also, who the main people are who influence the decision makers.

Representative: I could be convinced that I'm missing something there. But it's still not enough incentive to get married.

Manager: Let's take the second process, an account's basic operating process. If you don't know a customer's operating methods and policies, you can't know his cost burdens because that's where they pile up. And if you don't know where his operating costs are concentrated—whether it is in his distribution process, manufacturing, administrative processes, or whatever—then you can't sell our products and services to him as ways of reducing those costs. You're leaving money on the table that could be ours.

Representative: O.K., so I know some of his costs, but I don't know all. If I'm leaving money, I'm still taking a fair share in proportion to my time and effort. What's wrong with that?

Manager: The customer's third process is unavailable to you, that's what. And it's the most promising process for our purposes: his profit-making process. How does this customer make money? What are his best-selling products and services, the 20% that give him up to 80% of his profitable sales volume? How can we help him make even more money on his winners through the use of our products and services? You have to become partners with him to learn all that; you need to know about his profit. One thing is sure: He's never going to tell you about this if you are just one of many suppliers on his list.

Representative: But if I get more deeply involved to the point of partnership, all we'll have is family fights. He'll want lower prices on everything. I'll want higher ones. What kind of basis for marriage is that?

Manager: The wrong one. Try this instead: A business partnership must be based on making mutual profit. That's what you must do in common. Be a joint profit-improvement team. Think of yourselves as the "Bottom-Line Boys" or the "Profit-Improvement Patrol." Look for opportunities to sell into his decision-making process in ways that reduce the costs of his operating processes and help increase his profit on sales. If you keep the focus on mutual profit enhancement, prices will become secondary.

Representative: If this is such a great way to work with customers, there must be a special name for salespeople who do it.

Manager: There is. I call it being a profit-improvement consultant who is married to the customer.

Representative: What if it's to more than one customer?

Manager: Well, you just have to become a profit-improvement bigamist.

6
Price Protection

Holding Margins by Converting Price into an Investment

When Price Becomes an Insurmountable Problem, Try Giving the Product Away

Asking for a price makes customers defensive because price is a cost. But asking for an investment promises a return—a chance to make money instead of spending it.

Sales representative: I lost my third sale in a row this week and all for the same reason: We were underbid. You've got to give us more latitude on price.

Field sales manager: How much would you like?

Representative: As much as we need to meet competition. If you want a specific number, I'd say 20% to 30% more.

Manager: I'll do better than that. I'll give you 100% latitude on price.

Representative: 100%? You mean we can quote any price we want to?

Manager: Any price you want to, down to and including zero.

Representative: Zero price? You mean we can give the product away free?

Manager: Free, with my compliments.

Representative: But we'll go out of business that way.

Manager: Exactly. And that's just what we're doing. We're going out of business as a scale manufacturer at the close of the working day.

Representative: You mean I'm through here?

Manager: No, quite the contrary. You're just beginning here. We're going out of the scale business and we're entering a new business of improving customers' profits by reducing the costs of their weighing and quality-control operations.

Representative: That sounds like a service business. All of my experience is with tangibles.

191

Manager: What's more tangible than a customer's profit? He can touch it, measure it, take it to the bank. You don't think that a customer's bank account is composed of intangibles, do you?

Representative: What about the scales that we're going to be giving away at zero price: Is this a closeout?

Manager: Just the opposite. I expect we'll be selling more scales than ever before. The main difference is that I'm going to take your suggestion about price latitude to heart and give you all you want. After all, if 30% latitude will increase our sales somewhat, 100% latitude should increase sales a whole lot more. And giving our scales away at no price at all should enable us to sew up the market, right?

Representative: Sure. But just tell me how we're going to make enough money to pay my salary, will you?

Manager: I'm glad you asked. Let's role-play it. You're in front of the customer. "Mr. Hanan," (just to take a name out of the air)" you're saying, "I'm your company's consultant in *improving profit* by reducing the cost of your weighing operations." Please notice how I said that. Also notice what I didn't say: "I'm selling scales." What I presented is the *end benefit* of scales.

Representative: You also presented me differently. You changed me from a salesman into a consultant.

Manager: Right. "Now, Mr. Hanan, as your profit-improvement consultant, my job is to affect your bottom line. If I can help you speed up your weighing functions, I can reduce a cost to you. If I can help you increase the accuracy of your weighing, I can save you additional money by preventing overfilling—and also underfilling, which can lead to expensive makeup shipments and loss of goodwill and customer confidence. By my preliminary calculations, I believe I can save you about $500,000 a year in processing-time costs, product cost, goodwill costs, and costs of customer maintenance," All right, what am I selling?

Representative: Profit improvement. When do you sell the scales?

Manager: Hang in. "Now, Mr. Hanan, this $500,000 I can save you isn't just a one-time saving. It will be saved year after year, forever. Now here's my proposition. Is it worth three years of those savings for me to help you achieve them? In other words, is it worth $1.5 million to you to save $500,000 a year through infinity?"

Representative: "Sure. After three years, all my savings are net."

Manager: "That's good thinking. Now, Mr. Hanan, the $1.5 million I'm asking for is a professional fee for my consulting services. They include my homework to identify the nature and size of your weighing cost center, prescribing an optional system to reduce that cost, managing the installation of the system and teaching your people how to operate and maintain it, helping you measure its productivity, and upgrading the system over time."

Representative: But you didn't say anything about selling the scales.

Manager: I'm not going to. "As a bonus with my professional services, Mr. Hanan, I'm going to give you, absolutely free, our most sophisticated electronic scale system." Now here's my question: What's the price of the scales?

Representative: There is no price. It's included in the fee.

Manager: That's one way to look at it. Here's another. The customer isn't paying *us*. We're paying *him*. He's making $1 million within five years by doing business with us. He makes, not spends, money by doing business with us. His purchases become an investment, not a cost.

Representative: On that basis, why would he ever want to buy a scale from our competitors?

Manager: (weighing his answer carefully): Strange, but I can't think of any reason.

Before You Affect a Customer's Price Upward, Think How You Can Affect His Value Even More

If price is what the customer gives up, the first question we must answer is, What does he get in return? More is always better.

Field sales manager: What's the thing you dread most about selling?

Sales representative: Getting complaints. No, there's something even worse: notifying a customer of a price increase.

Manager: Why is that the worst?

Representative: No matter how I do it, I look bad and feel bad. I'm bringing bad news with nothing to offset it. It's going to cost a customer more money to do business with me, that's all there is to it. And because the pricing of his company's product is at least partly based on my price, I feel bad about his profits.

Manager: But you've been trained to handle price objections, haven't you?

Representative: To handle them, yes. But to deal with them responsibly, no. How would you like to be "handled" if you had a problem?

Manager: Maybe we ought to review how you perceive your sales training.

Representative: I'm doing exactly what I've been trained to do. I relate our price rise to need: our need to recover our own increased costs. In my most recent apology, I had three cost increments to lean on. Our own raw materials costs had gone up, our labor costs had just risen under our new contract at the plant, and our new investment in environmental protection, which is totally nonproductive, had to be passed along. How's that?

Manager: Why were you apologizing? Almost every company's costs in those categories have gone up as much as ours, even more. Besides, we've been the best company in the industry in absorbing cost increases. So why think of yourself as apologizing?

Representative: Because, in effect, I'm asking a customer for more money without offering him any more value in return.

Manager: Suppose you were actually able to show greater value; how would you feel about it then?

Representative: A lot better. But how am I going to show greater value from our pollution-control investments? Perhaps I should tell the customer he can now breathe cleaner air while he signs our inflated purchase order.

Manager: How do you think of the value you're supplying right now in return for your present price? What are you giving for what you're getting?

Representative: A lot. High-quality product, excellent quality control, on-time delivery, favorable terms, applications services furnished free of charge. But the customer's already paying for all that right now. That's what we mean by a fair price, isn't it?

Manager: If you stop there, yes. Aren't there any other values you can sell? Let's call them added values that can justify an added price.

Representative: I can't find any. That's why I don't want to go in to a customer with a higher price, unless I can bring something to the party that's worth paying for.

Manager: Let's think the way the customer does and see if we can find something we give him that's worth paying more for. Don't give me any answers that have to do with our product or service, O.K.? Now tell me how we affect customer value.

Representative: Well, I suppose ultimately we affect his bottom line.

Manager: Right, but how?

Representative: One way is that our product helps the customer's product perform better. That helps him sell more of his product—perhaps even charge a higher price for it or make repeat sales that keep his selling costs down.

Manager: Stop right there. So far, you've said three things:

1. We add value to a customer by helping improve his profit.

2. We can improve customer profit by helping him increase his sales.
3. We can improve customer profit still another way, by helping him reduce his costs.

As generalities, those are great. Can you give me some specifics?

Representative: Sure. There must be dozens of ways we can affect a customer's profit. We can help with his inventory control, reduce his operating costs by training his people to perform better, or help his manufacturing scheduling. In fact, we can make an even earlier impact by helping his product development people.

Manager: All right, all right. That's enough for a start. If you do only one or two of those things, you should have enough to keep you busy—and selling—for a long time to come. Now, let's get back to the problem we started with. If you really believe that you can help improve a customer's profit, why should you dread announcing a price increase? Is the customer buying our price, or is he buying our ability to help improve his profit?

Representative: Our ability, of course. So when our price increases, my job is to make sure that our ability increases along with it, or even exceeds it. The customer will pay more, but he'll get more value for his money. Do I have it right?

Manager: The best way to tell whether you have it right is by how you feel. Do you *feel* right about it?

Representative: When's our next price increase?

Don't Send a New Product to Market Naked, with Its Margins Exposed— Protect It with a System

"I thought the whole idea with a new product was to saturate a market with it as quickly as possible—to get it through the distribution pipeline and into every customer's hands as fast as possible," the sales manager says to the president. "Now you tell me I'm doing it all wrong, that I'm making instant commodities out of all our big winners by sacrificing margin to get volume. So where do I go from here?"

"Go to daylight, to profits," the president responds, "and don't stop until you cross the bottom line."

The expression "sunk costs" has more meaning today than ever before. These are all the investment costs that must be sunk into a new product before it enters the market: the cost of inventing it, engineering it, manufacturing it, testing it, advertising it, and distributing it—all before a penny of revenues starts coming back. Inflation, the increasing costs of new technologies, and the ability of competition to come on strong quickly push every one of these expenses higher every year.

Thus it is understandable that getting to the first moment of payback is on everyone's mind. One of the most popular strategies is called "introductory pricing." It encourages people to buy at once. Unfortunately, however, it also encourages people to define the new product as a price brand.

"Sure," the president says, "we want to get our investment back. Otherwise we'll go broke. But if that's all we do with each new product, I'll be out of a job and so will you. Nobody goes through all that work with something new just to break even."

"That's why we price attractively right off the bat," the sales manager argues. "We give deals and discounts, even premiums, just to get a product in place with customers."

"You get us revenues that way, all right. But what about getting some earnings on them? When you start out by giving away half of our legitimate margins, there's not going to be much left to give away when the competition starts to imitate us. That's what I mean when I talk about instant commodities. You set a price standard that normally comes about over time, after we've had a chance to enjoy good margins as our reward for being the innovator."

"But the reward for being the innovator at a high introductory price is to slow down trial and acceptance," the sales manager says. "We may impress the market with our leadership, but will we impress our financial people who want to replace their red ink with black?"

The history of low introductory prices suggests that they stay that way. Only rarely does an entry price move upward over time. The only way out is to "make it up in volume." But that usually adds further costs to the product for added plant capacity, increased distribution costs, sales costs, advertising costs—all the costs that are necessary to support a market saturation campaign.

"What about the history of premium prices at introduction?" the sales manager says. "They extend to every competitor an engraved invitation that says, in effect, 'Come on in, the water's fine.' "

"When we come in low we have no competitors, is that what you're saying? Fine. Then let's reduce the prices of all our products 50% across the board and get rid of the whole lot of them."

Faced with the dilemma of paying off heavy investments or maintaining premium margins, companies are "planning backward." Before a new product is launched, they look ahead a year or two and try to figure out how to postpone the inevitable erosion of margins as long as possible.

"Never mind new products for the moment," the president says. "Take an older one that has become a commodity because it is mature. Let's say our competitors have perfect replicas of it. All of us are selling just above cost because none of us can think of any way to differentiate ourselves. How do you deal with that?"

"I protect the product," the sales manager responds quickly. "As soon as it becomes vulnerable as a stand-alone item (in other words, when both our customers and our competitors start to go to work on us to bring down the price) I tuck it into a system. I shelter it with services and with our expert knowledge of a customer's business or of the requirements of his own customers that we can help him meet. I also bundle into the same package a financial plan that lets him have better terms than we ordinarily make available, or I include a rental option on some of our products that otherwise he'd have to purchase. Oh, yes, there's our training package, which I also include. I price the system as a whole, not the product that's somewhere inside it. And I price it on the basis of the contribution we calculate it can make to the improvement of his profit."

"And what does all that accomplish?" the president asks.

"It gives us the chance to raise price without raising price."

"Well, then," the president says, "why don't you do the same thing *before* a product becomes a commodity? That will keep it from becoming one."

Protecting new products by protecting their price is a well-proven benefit of systems. Even though the product's performance characteristics may be imitated by competitors or evaluated on a price-performance basis by customers (more and more performance for less and less price), the system can still command a high margin because its value is connected to customer profit.

"Now how do you feel about gaining initial customer acceptance with a new product . . . excuse me, I mean a new system?" the president asks.

"I'm wondering who will be more surprised, our customers or our competitors."

"That's easy," says the president. "If you're any indication, it will be our own people. You'd better get busy."

When You're a Strong No. 2, Give the Customer a Strong Reason to Change from No. 1

"Being No. 1 means one thing most of all," the sales manager tells his assembled honchos. "Depending on the industry you're in, it means you're on the approved list, on the shelf, installed, imbedded in the specs. Emplacement—the name of the game—has already occurred. If you're No. 2, as we are, the problem is simple to define but difficult to execute. Our game is displacement. Now, how are we going to go about doing it?"

All the regional managers have the answer on the tips of their tongues. It's easy: price. Buy your way in. But the sales manager makes it difficult.

"I want to displace number one *without* sacrificing our margins or our image as a quality house. As a matter of fact, I want to gain new share at a premium price. Now what answers do you have?"

Taking on the industry leader without a significant price advantage is not the traditional way of breaking into a leader's franchise, either in your own market or when penetrating a new market segment. But it is on the rise as the way things are going to be done in the 1990s for a very good reason: Market share gained at the expense of profit is becoming increasingly unaffordable. Margins that are given away up front, as a down payment to get in, may never be recovered regardless of later volume. Nor may the image as a price brand ever be eradicated.

Free trial is always a popular suggestion. In reality, it may be the ultimate price offer: no price. If sampling is to work, however, it should be planned with two considerations in mind. First, when follow-on sales are made, they must be made at a premium price. Second, the sampled trial must be positioned as the forerunner of a more comprehensive strategy. What is it?

With price ruled out, the regional managers are quiet. They are coming to grips with a basic marketing truism: One of the reasons so many leading companies retain their leadership is not strategic brilliance on their part but an absence of displacement strategies on the part of their competitors.

But this sales manager thinks he has a solution by the tail and he wants to swing it across the collective consciousness of his regional managers. Pointing to one of them, he says, "Role-play with me. You be the customer. No. 1 is your major supplier. Why?"

" 'Quality product. Acceptable price. Good service.' Quality, price, and service. So what else is new?"

"Once these reasons to buy become established," the sales manager says, "they become standardized, right? They become expected, insisted on, the norm. You don't want to lose them so you have no incentive to change. Why else won't you change?"

"No reason to," one of the regional managers says. "That's the flip side of not wanting to risk what you have. It's not seeing any greater rewards from the other guys."

"We know one thing if we know anything about selling," the sales manager says. "No reason to change is the most prevalent reason why change does not take place. So what does that tell us?"

"We need a reason. That's what price does—it provides a reason."

"Wrong," the sales manager says. "It avoids a reason. It admits there is no real reason to change: no unique benefits, no perform-ance advantages, no attributes that cannot be obtained elsewhere. All it does is offer comparable attributes made cheaper. Are we willing to acknowledge that our product is only comparable to the leader's?"

"No way!" the regional managers chorus. "We are the innova-tor. We are the leading edge. We're the breakthrough."

"All right," says the sales manager. "Be the customer again. You're fat and happy doing business with No. 1; notice I did not say fat, dumb, and happy. Do you have any concerns at all? Any fears, any doubts, anything I can exploit?"

"If we're using No. 1 exclusively—or even if it's only largely— maybe we have a concern. How would it go? 'Am I using No. 1 too much, in too many places, in the wrong places where it's not cost-effective for me, where something else would give me a better return? Would I be better off to be selective, at least in some very important respects?' "

"Exactly," the sales manager says. "In one word, what is the object of your concern?"

"My mix."

"Your mix—the thing that you as a customer come to work to monitor, to conduct like an orchestra leader so that it is in harmony with . . . what?"

"Cost-effectiveness," says one regional manager.

"Profits," says another.

"My own sales," says a third.

Each of them is correct.

"Now," the sales manager says, "I want you to correct the sampling strategy to a strategy of fine-tuning the customer's mix. The idea is to sample in the very areas where you believe it will make the most significant improvement in the performance of his mix according to the criteria you've just enunciated. There's just one missing ingredient. Anyone?"

"Whatever happened to premium price?"

"That's it. Do you see now how you can justify it?"

"Sure," a manager says. "If I can prove to my customer that I can boost the performance of his mix in specific dollar terms, why can't I charge him a premium, based on the costs I've saved him or the new profits I'm helping him make?"

"So what do we come out with?" the sales manager asks. "In the apparent absence of a reason to change suppliers, we give the customer a reason to change something else: his mix. But it's not really his mix he wants to change. It's the return he's getting from it. If we can improve the return, we can displace the leader. Would anyone like to take a crack at the final question? What are we really giving a customer the chance to do?"

Now the answers come. "Make more money with us."

"Save money by doing business with us."

"Improve his own operations with our help."

The last answer ends the meeting: "Pay us a premium price. Don't laugh, there's no opportunity for him to do that with No. 1."

While You're Justifying Your Cost, the Customer Knows That No Cost Is Justifiable

Every time you try to justify your cost, you go on the defensive. You hand over the initiative to the customer, who will quite naturally take advantage of it to bring your cost down even lower.

General sales manager: So what's this new program you've been getting everybody excited about out in your region?

Regional sales manager: You've probably heard the theme: If it's price-sensitive, cost-justify it. I think we'll have a winner with it. What do you think?

General SM: I'll give you a good grade for the concept. But your choice of language is atrocious. I hope you won't ever use words like that in my presence again. Cost! Justification! I should wash your mouth out with soap.

Regional SM: What's the matter with them? Our price is a cost to the customer, isn't it? And when the customer complains about the cost, how can we sell him unless we can justify the expense as representing the least cost?

General SM: It's a defeatist way to sell. Let's take it apart and examine it. The theme of this little exercise will be something like this: When you cost-justify, you really cost-dramatize. You do the very thing you try to avoid.

Regional SM: If that's true, then there's no way to sell against a price objection. Remember what we're faced with. We have a good product, but so do our competitors. We have some features and benefits they don't have. They have others we don't have. Some of our salespeople are better than theirs. Some of theirs are better than ours. We've all priced ourselves down to the bone. So what's left to sell but the claim that we do the least damage to the customer's checkbook?

General SM: I prefer the flip side of that claim: that we do the most good for the customer's bank account.

Regional SM: But that sounds as if we're going to make money for him instead of saving what he already has.

General SM: We are. That's what you're missing out on by concentrating on cost. If we save him costs, we automatically make money for him. A penny saved is a penny earned, right?

Regional SM: So you're saying we should concentrate on the end benefit of cost saving instead of the feature that makes it possible. What do we want to call it?

General SM: How about profit improvement?

Regional SM: You don't like profit justification?

General SM: That's one of the differences between cost and profit. You always have to justify a cost, even when it's lower than a cost you're replacing. Somebody still has to pay for it. But nobody ever has to justify a profit.

Regional SM: So selling profit, which everybody wants, is more aggressive than selling a justified cost that nobody wants in the first place, is that it? But how do we prove profit? We're having a hard enough time justifying cost, if you'll pardon the expression.

General SM: I won't. But let's go on anyway. How are you justifying cost right now?

Regional SM: First we try to find out what it's costing now for a customer to solve a certain problem or operate a given function. Then we cost out his options. These include our competition. Finally we cost out our own solution. If we come out lowest, we sell ourselves as being the most justifiable vendor. Even if we're close, we can try to make a case for ourselves.

General SM: Let's turn things around. Instead of trying to be lowest, let's try to be highest—highest in the profit we can deliver to a customer rather than lowest in cost.

Regional SM: We've been trying to quantify the cost benefit. Can we do the same with profit?

General SM: Almost exactly. You still need to know your customer's present costs and the costs of his available solutions. (By the way, that's not a bad definition of a competitor: another available solution.) Then you figure out your impact on the customer. If you can save him more than his current cost, the difference can be interpreted to him in terms of profit. The same goes for the difference between our cost and the expense of a competitive solution.

Regional SM: Sometimes we can eliminate a whole category of cost. What then?

General SM: Cost elimination goes right to the bottom line of the customer's business as profits. To eliminate a cost category instead of just reducing it is one of the most important benefits we can confer on a customer. It's like taking one step out of a process, reducing energy requirements, or permanently reducing labor.

Regional SM: O.K., so I go back and retrain my teams of cost justifiers to be profit improvers. Is there anything else we should be on the lookout for in our new role as improvers?

General SM: There are two ways to improve a customer's profit, you know. Cost reduction or removal is one of them. The other is increasing a customer's sales by what we sell him. Are you being alert to our opportunities there?

Regional SM: Our customers get a higher-quality product as a result of doing business with us. More dependable delivery dates because of reduced downtime. And some aspects of our ability to reduce costs allow a customer to reduce or maintain his own price so that he can give better value. Things like that?

General SM: How many of these benefits can you convert into dollar figures? That will take homework to find out. Once you do, you can add these dollar values to the profit effects of cost reduction and come out with an even bigger number. That's what you should be selling instead of justified cost.

Regional SM: Is that the distinction you were making between cost justification being defensive and profit improvement being a more aggressive sell?

General SM: Exactly. For a businessman, profit is . . . what's that famous old saying that everybody learns as a child but forgets as soon as he starts to sell?

Regional SM: Profits, the name of the game? I'm going to paraphrase something you said earlier that I'd like to challenge. "I like the concept, but not your language." We can talk cost with anybody we call on. Purchasing agents, engineers, function managers, operating people. But how many of them understand profit? If they don't, we could end up talking to ourselves.

General SM: That's right. So you have three options. One is to go on talking cost to people who are responsible for costs and have absolutely no connection with people who are responsible for profits. The second is to train other customer decision makers to think profit and to communicate it upward into higher levels of management. The third is the one I would really like to see you get into. Revise your entry points higher into the decision-maker ranks of your key account customers. They'll know what you're talking about. Think you can do it?

Regional SM: After our little talk, I feel somewhat more—how shall I say it?—boss-justified.

When a Premium Is Placed on Premium Pricing, Premium Profits Are the Result

The difference between selling volume and selling profits is a good deal more than academic. To make it real, it ought to show up in the quota system and the reward system as well.

General sales manager: How familiar are you with the critical ratios in a business—what they are, what they mean?

Regional sales manager: They're comparisons, aren't they? They let managers compare sets of decisions that have a direct relationship to each other. The one I think of first is ROI, comparing return with the investment spent to make it.

General SM: ROI is a good example. So is profit on sales, comparing your volume with what we make on it. Both of these ratios are bothering me more and more about our performance. Investment keeps rising, but return isn't increasing in proportion. Volume holds or even grows, but profits decline. Where does it all end?

Regional SM: If we're not careful, we can end up owning all the volume in the industry but going broke, right?

General SM: That may be a bit dramatic, but you've got the point. Volume is a cost. So the question I spend a lot of my time on these days is this one: How can we increase our profit on sales?

Regional SM: Sell more. Isn't it that simple?

General SM: If it were, we'd both be in the field sales force instead of managing. Selling more will increase revenues. But if the costs of selling more make the profits increasingly marginal, we still haven't increased our profits on sales enough to make it a good deal.

Regional SM: Then there's only one other answer. Raise

prices—oh, I know what you'll tell me. Raise our price and volume goes down. So we're right back where we began.

General SM: Maybe not. It depends on two things: what we raise prices on and what added value we offer in return for the higher price.

Regional SM: That used to be called selective pricing.

General SM: It still is. And I'm about to select it as the basis of our sales policy from now on. The way I'm going to do it is to create a new critical ratio and make everybody responsible for it.

Regional SM: High-priced offerings compared to what, low prices?

General SM: Essentially. But I'm going to dress it up a little. I'm going to establish two sets of prices. One is premium price. That will give us a high profit per sale. Everything else is promoted price.

Regional SM: The sales force is full of ingenious people, you know. Give them two categories of anything, and they'll find a way to do most of their business in a third classification they'll invent for themselves.

General SM: If they do, it will be for another company, not this one. But I appreciate the point and I think I know how to prevent the problem. I'm going to impose as a standard of their performance the ratio of premium-priced sales to promoted sales. But I'm going to let each of them tell me the best ratio he thinks he can come up with and what his premium-priced products will be. I'm going to hold him to both commitments.

Regional SM: What you're talking about comes under the headings of participation and entrapment—I mean commitment. Would that be stating the case accurately?

General SM: Not just accurately but heart-warmingly. Do you suppose I can expect the same understanding from your people?

Regional SM: You're asking them to act like business managers in a way: to be profit-conscious, to evaluate their lines, and to make a kind of forecast of where their main profit contributions will come from. It's hard to argue against in theory.

General SM: It's going to be even harder for them to argue against in practice. Each sales representative will set a series of quotas for himself. First, he'll decide that, say, 40% of his total volume will be in promoted sales. Then he should be able to tell you that these sales will come from the following products: All of Lines A, B, and C, plus Line D when sold to Market X only. The rest of the Line D sales will be premium-priced to Markets Y and Z at all times. Once a sales representative puts a product line on the premium-priced list, it will take your signature to get it off. I retain the right of veto.

Regional SM: You'll need more than just that statement, though, won't you? What about change over time? I have people doing 70% of their sales at what you call promotional prices: deals, discounts, giveaways of one kind or another. In that situation, don't you want a commitment to get the ratio of premium-priced sales to promoted sales up from 30:70 to 50:50 in a year or so and eventually to tip it to 60:40?

General SM: Maybe. It depends on the product and the markets. In our commodity lines, where we have mature, me-too products with tough price competition, certain products will always have to be promoted. But others don't. I want our people to recognize the difference between products that must be lowballed and those that give us the opportunity to win premium prices despite their commodity status.

Regional SM: That's where the competence of our salespeople comes in: whether we can master the strategies of selling some type of premium value along with the product so that we can justify a premium price.

General SM: The most important thing is that we improve our profits. Some of our people can do that for us by selling more premium-priced offerings. That obviously raises our margins. Other salespeople can help our profits by selling promoted-price lines more cost-effectively by knowing what they are doing and why they are doing it. So the second most important thing is that we improve our knowledge of what we sell and to whom.

Regional SM: So you're not saying that the people who sell the premium-priced lines will inherit the earth—and it's tough luck for the performance-price peddlers?

General SM: Not at all, as long as each improves his profit on sales by keeping my new critical ratio in the forefront of his sales strategy. But do you know who my real favorites are going to be?

Regional SM: The ones who make the most impressive turna-rounds from 60% promoted to 60% premium?

General SM: Well, they'll be in my inner circle for sure. I was thinking of a slightly different kind of achievement, though. How about the salesperson who finds a way to take a promoted offering and convert it to premium status? That, I think, is the purest form of selling skill. That says someone not only knows the *what*—the difference between volume and profits—he also knows the *how* of increasing the profits even when the volume remains steady. My crown prince, of course, will be the salesperson who can increase both.

Regional SM: Have you calculated the critical ratio of that kind of salesperson in our organization?

General SM: This year I'll settle for 30%, next year 50%, and in three years 100%.

Regional SM: From Training 101, I'd say that would be close to miraculous.

General SM: Then may I suggest that, since you now know the curriculum, you move your people pronto into Training 102.

When You Take On the Price Leader, Charge Even Higher—and Make Your Value Higher Still

A lower price may not say anything definitive about value. But a higher price always does—as long as the value backs it up.

Field sales manager (addressing the sales force): In a few minutes, I'm going to introduce you to our new product. We're going to use it to take on No. 1 head to head. I'll tell you two things about it, then I'd like your suggestions about our sales strategy. First, we will not price aggressively. In other words, we will not buy our way in. Second, we have a product that is no different from any other on the market. Does anyone have any questions before we proceed?

1st sales rep: Why are we getting into a market where we have to take on a financially strong, entrenched competitor who's got the experience curve working for him?

Manager: Three reasons: There's a slow rate of technical change in the industry, and we can cash in on that. There's a low breakeven point we think we can reach quickly. And only a 3% to 5% market share in the first year can yield us a profit.

2nd rep: I wish we didn't have just a parity product. Doesn't it have any unique performance benefits at all?

Manager: No. It's totally undifferentiated. I told you that technical change was slow.

3rd rep: Then why aren't we coming in as the low-price supplier? How can we justify a fully competitive price?

Manager: That's what I want *you* to tell *me*.

2nd rep: We could give it a catchy brand name that implies an unusual benefit.

Manager: The product manager has decided to give it an alphanumeric designation. You know, like the SX-70.

211

1st rep: Sell service instead of the product.

Manager: Do you mean charge for it? Or feature it as our strong point and give it away with the product?

1st rep: Charge for it.

Manager: Why will customers pay for our service when they already get No. 1's service free? Remember, you pointed out that our big competitor has the experience curve going for him. How could we compete?

1st rep: All right. Then let's give away our service.

Manager: I've already said we will not buy our way in. Giving away service is a hidden price offer.

4th rep: How about coming in with a parity product but then innovating continually?

Manager: I mentioned the rather low breakeven point in our penetration of this industry. As soon as we invest in innovation, our breakeven rises. By innovating continually we might never make a profit. Don't forget that this is a low-growth technology area. What could we innovate?

5th rep: You've probably got an answer to this one, too, but I'll try it anyway. How about coming out with a broad product line—a full line, maybe—instead of just a single product?

Manager: There go our costs again. Do you realize the incremental expenditures required to develop, test, manufacture, and market even a two-product line? We'll have a broad line sometime, but not at first. It's a matter of economics.

3rd rep: You've got an objection to everything we suggest. So I'll just make one more recommendation. What do you say we just buy No. 1?

Manager: Very funny. Now, what we're really going to do actually consists of three things. The first is to get to know our potential customers' business. What aspects in particular?

4th rep: The first thing I'd go after is a knowledge of every key customer's cost structure insofar as our new product can affect him: his purchasing costs, inventory costs, manufacturing and assembly costs, and right through to his sales costs. Maybe we can lower them because he's using our product instead of someone else's.

Manager: That's one half of the equation. What other aspect of our customer's business do we have to get to know?

5th rep: I'd vote for knowledge of how his own customers do business with him and how we can help him step up his sales to them. Knowledge about his sales process is just as important as knowing about his manufacturing.

Manager: All right, let's say you get into your customer's business deep enough to learn how to cut his costs and increase his sales as a result of doing business with us. What are you going to do with what you know?

1st rep: Sell to him on the basis of one of these two reasons to buy from us. Either we can help him reduce his costs more than the other guy, or we can help him increase his sales. That's why he should buy from us.

Manager: Suppose No. 1 does the same thing?

2nd rep: Is he?

Manager: Not yet, but he can.

2nd rep: If we do it best, then he's No. 2.

Manager: What are we doing for our customers by taking a cost-cutting, sales-raising approach with them? What's the net effect?

Chorus: We're adding to their value.

Manager: What value?

3rd rep: The value they get from dealing with us: the bottom-line value of improved profit.

Manager: That leaves the third and final consideration in our strategy, How do we add to our own value?

4th rep: By selling as much as we can to every customer while maintaining our price.

Manager: So it's not just volume, is it? It's volume at maintained prices. How do we do that?

2nd rep: We can't spend time making individual item sales, that's for sure. We'll have to sell systems composed of our new product plus other products that go with it. Or we'll put together a service package as the second part of our system. That's the best way to get volume sales without giving away price.

Manager: Do you have enough faith in our approach to take on No. 1 without lowering price? And instead use knowledge of our customer's business to sell systems that can help improve his bottom line?

5th rep: What better way is there? If we go in as the cheapie, we admit right off the bat that we're No. 2. But if we help customers make more money, there's greater value—not just lower cost—in doing business with us.

Manager: Any final questions about our pricing policy?

1st rep: Instead of just maintaining price, why can't we be the highest-priced supplier?

Manager: Now you're talking!

There's a Price to Being a Vendor, and You Always Pay It in Price

If you're a vendor competing against other vendors, the cost of competitive selling can be very high. But the hidden cost is the price a vendor pays in price.

Sales representative: I'm having trouble positioning myself as a consultant. Even my new title of account representative doesn't seem to help. My customers still treat me as a vendor. All they want to talk about is price.

Field sales manager: Some of that's the fault of those who have preceded you. We taught your customers all too well how to treat us as commodities vendors who sell on price. But my advice to you is still the same: Rise above it. Otherwise, you'll always pay the price in price.

Representative: When you told me that before, you said to do what a good pilot does: take off fast with a new image and climb high. But old images persist. I'm stuck at the bottom of that pyramid you drew.

Manager: As long as you continue to operate down there, you identify yourself as just another supplier. It's automatic. The only thing you can do is react to a purchaser's search for a set of exact specifications—at the lowest price. How can you be consultative that way?

Representative: I've tried to become the purchasing agent's buddy, to tell him what I know about the industry, to help him find ways to reduce costs so that he can come up with impressive savings for his management. But he keeps telling me that the best way I can help reduce his costs is to give him my lowest price. I'm right back to being a vendor again.

Manager: No matter how discouraging it is or how long it takes, keep on teaching him things he needs to know. Show him ways other than price deals to lower his costs. At the same time,

215

you've got to work your way up the pyramid to where you can be more consultative.

Representative: You mean go around the purchasing agent?

Manager: Not unless you absolutely have to, and then only with the greatest care. No, what I'm saying is to work *through* the purchasing agent, not around him. That way, both of you can move up the pyramid. He may not want to make the trip with you, but you've got to give him the chance.

Representative: How can I motivate him?

Manager: With benefits to him. Does he want management recognition? More power? Promotion along his career path? You're a seller. Sell him.

Representative: If I get him to move up one more level with me, how much better off am I as a consultant?

Manager: You're still not where you should be, but you're better off. When he reaches the next level above you, you can at least consult on how your product's technical specifications can contribute benefits in a more profitable manner than competitive products. That's applications consulting. It's not full-blown consultative selling, but it's better than being a vendor.

Representative: What you're saying, however, is that even at that level I would be reacting to the customer's solution. I'm still not providing him with my own solution, right?

Manager: Unfortunately, yes. If you want to sell solutions rather than applications expertise or product-at-a-price, you have to rise above the pyramid's second level and go all the way to the top.

Representative (reflectively): By working with the purchasing agent, rather than going around him.

Manager: Right. Remember, it's his company. He has access almost everywhere inside it. You don't. Here's the trade-off you have to make with him: I'll reward you with such benefits as knowledge, top management attention, or better performance; you reward me with access upstairs.

Representative: Do purchasing agents generally understand the significance of that kind of bargain?

Manager: You may have to explain that the top of the pyramid is where problems are first perceived. If you can get up there, you can help analyze them; you can sell your own solutions to them, building in our products and applications expertise. Just make it clear that it's not just products that you are selling, but solutions.

Representative: And that's what a consultant is: someone who perceives customer problems and sells solutions to them.

Manager: Beautifully said. You left out just one thing. The consultative salesman perceives customer problems *in terms of their effect on profit* and sells solutions to them.

Representative: And he trades off profit against high price. That way, the customer's objections to paying a higher price may be overcome by the chance to earn an even higher profit on his sales.

Manager: If you think like that, you're beginning to position yourself as a consultant.

Representative: And that's what you mean by "paying the price in price" if I remain a vendor. I'm not giving the customer any promise of higher profit, so he does the only thing he can to improve his profit by himself: force my price down as low as he can get it.

Manager: In that context, how do you measure the value added by consultation?

Representative: It's the difference between the consultant's price and the vendor's.

Manager: And what is it from the customer's point of view?

Representative: He sees it as the difference between the consultants' contribution to improved profit and his own ability to bargain for a lower price.

Manager: Right. And if your contribution can't be greater than his, well, you deserve to be a vendor.

Representative: Or a purchasing agent.

If the Customer Mentions the Cost, You've Lost

The general sales manager is getting severe with his account managers. He says, "You see it in baseball, especially with the pitcher when the count is 3 and 2. You see it in football with the quarterback on third down. You see it in politics when the heads of state go eyeball to eyeball and neither of them wants to be the first to blink. I'm talking about *control*. Tell me, how can you tell you're the one who's in control in a selling situation?"

Most salespeople and their managers take it as gospel that they must control the selling situation. They must be the ones to focus the customer's attention on their product's features, functions, and benefits. They must be the ones to overcome objections and make trial closes. If the customer is allowed to get a word in edgewise, they fear that the word will be "no."

It's easy to understand the manager's surprise when one of his people gives him an answer that he has never heard before. "I can never tell that I'm in control," the salesperson says, "because I'm never in control."

"Why not?" the manager asks.

"Oh, don't worry," the man says quickly. "I'm not out of control. But I'm never in control. I find I sell much better when I put the customer in control."

"How can you justify saying that?" the manager asks. "You're challenging hundreds of years of sales history. If we let the customer dominate the sales call, we'll end up giving our product away."

"My experience says something else," the salesman replies. "When I used to control my calls, I started talking about my product from the minute I walked through the customer's door. Features, functions, and benefits. Price and performance. Specs, and why ours were always better. My calls always ended up the same way. The customer would ask me, 'How much?' When I'd tell him, he'd say, 'Too much.' I learned something from that: if the customer mentions the cost, I've lost. Oh, maybe not the sale. But the margin."

"And that always happened when you controlled the sale by talking product?" the manager asks. "You're saying that the result of control is selling on price, that it all comes down to price when you take command of the sale right from the start?"

"Yes, and I think I know why. I was the one who set the theme: my product. I was the one who controlled the dialogue about my product's performance. So naturally the customer reacted to my leadership. What else could he react to? I forced him to get into my business, and I told him everything he needed to know about it and more, except the one thing he had to ask: my price. Then I either lost him or I lost our profit."

"So now what do you do," the manager asks, "to keep the customer from mentioning cost? What exactly do you mean that you're never in control?"

"I make every presentation with the objective of putting my customer in control," the salesman says. "I arrived at this by asking myself, What can the customer logically be in control of? It certainly can't be my product. I'm the expert in my product. So I figured he must be able to control his business if he couldn't be in control of mine. Then I began to ask around about who controlled the operation that I was selling into. When I found out, I let the customer talk to me about what he controlled."

"And what did you learn?"

"For starters, I learned that customers were a lot more comfortable talking about the operations they controlled, say, a manufacturing process or inventory functions, than they were about things that I controlled. They knew them better. So they were less defensive. Because they were in control, they taught me what they knew. That way, I learned a lot about new sales opportunities."

"Anything else?" the manager asks.

"I also learned where they were out of control: where their costs were too high or their productivity or sales were too low. Since they were the ones controlling our dialogue, they were relaxed enough to tell me what their deficiencies were as well as what they were proud of. So I learned even more about sales opportunities."

"But there must have come a time when you regained control, when you became assertive about your product and closed the sale, wasn't there? You just can't sit there and act like someone in an

audience while the customer goes on and on about what he controls," the manager says.

"I never want control," the salesman answers. "I can tell sometimes when I'm getting dangerously close to it because the customer
mentions my product's cost. That's an infallible sign, because it
means that I've been talking about my own business, trying to take
control away from the customer. So I put him back in control as fast
as I can."

"How do you do that?"

"By going back to talking about things the customer controls—
his costs, his productivity, and his operations and their problems and
opportunities. That way, I can ask him the question that I don't want
him to ask me: 'What's it costing you to pay for that inefficiency or
that scrap rate or that downtime?' When he tells me, that gives me
my sales target. Now I know what to shoot at."

"When he hears you mention cost," the manager asks, "doesn't
that signal him that he's lost control of the dialogue to you? Doesn't
it work both ways?"

"Sure it does," the salesman says. "But now it works in my favor.
Because I can help him reduce the expenses under his control, he's
the one who comes out with a lower cost, not me. That makes him
happy. He never mentions my cost. That makes me happy, especially
since I almost always come away with a higher price than I ever
would have gotten when I was the only one in control."

7

Customer Satisfaction

Making Sure the Product Works to Help the Customer Work Better

How Quickly Will You Answer When the Customer Squints at You and Asks, "Why Do We Need You Guys?"

Suppliers traditionally assume that a customer has three choices: buy it from us, buy it from a competitor, or do without it altogether. Now, buyers are contemplating three other options: make it ourselves, eliminate the part or process that we get from a supplier, or use a substitute.

There seem to be five major reasons why customers in a number of industries, consumer as well as industrial, are considering those options.

1. "Suppliers, even the best of them, have become unreliable," some customers say. "One week the materials we need are on allocation; the next week they want us to warehouse for them. Today, price has just gone up. When we ask for a commitment, they say price will be determined at delivery. Of course, by then it will be up again. Meanwhile, they're constantly changing the ground rules. Policy is a joke."

2. "We can't depend on our suppliers' quality control any more. When they can't get materials, they use a synthetic. Then they let us find out for them whether the new material works or not. Often it doesn't. Then the recalls come. The negative effect on *our own customers* is incalculable."

3. "They're all trying to reduce costs by concentrating on their most profitable lines. Everything else is being discontinued or divested. It's unfortunate that we need products that some of our major suppliers find less profitable to make. When we can't get them, we're thrown into the open market. Screening new suppliers is costly, dangerous, and uncomfortable."

4. "Everybody's cut back on inventories. Our suppliers don't

223

like to make anything anymore until they know they can sell it. There are fewer colors, sizes, shapes, styles, formulations, horsepowers—fewer everything. Immediate delivery is a thing of the past. They ship more slowly now, too; the bill usually gets here before the goods."

5. "They're cutting back on their sales forces. Coverage is thinner. Their top salespeople call only on what they classify as national accounts. Smaller customers get a dealer or distributor salesman, who often is a cut below what we're used to. We just don't have the same level of confidence."

For these reasons, customers are asking, Do we really need to do business this way? If the answer comes up no, the company can free itself from a whole set of problems that appear likely to get worse.

Ironically, it seems that relatively few suppliers are aware of that kind of customer thinking; it's too easy for suppliers to assume they will always be needed. But what would you say if a key account asked *you* the ultimate question? Could you answer it persuasively from the account's perspective, or would you just blurt out something about the value of past relationships? There are ways to think about counteracting the three major customer options.

1. When the customer wants to make it himself. When you come down to it, most businesses exist because someone else's make-or-buy decision came out "buy." Cost-effectiveness made it turn out that way. In many cases today, however, buying has become costly. It may be more efficient for a customer to control his own materials supply than have to put up with shortfalls, allocations, price spirals, and other uncertainties. For the first time in many industries, self-manufacture makes economic sense.

How can you counteract it? In the past, cost justification was the answer, but you will need more ammunition now. You may find that there are only two reasons why your customers should go on buying from you, neither of which has anything to do directly with your product.

One is the personal applications expertise of your salesmen. The other is the technical and marketing information base they have built up on how to use your product and services to improve customer profit. If you aren't selling those benefits now, consider them as your best bets to discourage self-manufacture.

2. The threat of having your component or process eliminated. Now we come to the opposite situation: a customer's decision to eliminate a component or process altogether. If that happens, you could find yourself cut off from an important account overnight. The customer may decide to buy a finished component or product from a subcontractor, or he may decide to omit an ingredient entirely. The dollar cost of going to a subassembler may be greater than the cost of doing business with you (at least initially), but it may be worth it in terms of improved security, comfort, and continuity of supply.

That is probably the most difficult kind of customer tactic to defend against. It is the acid test of your knowledge of a customer's business. If you argue from a cost-reduction or profit-improvement point of view, you will require current information about his direct and indirect manufacturing and processing costs. You will have to be sure that the costs net out in your favor when you compare them with the costs of buying finished components outside. What's more, you will have to go beyond cost considerations and solve the problem of ensuring uninterrupted supplies.

3. What to do when customers want to switch materials. As soon as a material comes into short supply, substitutes suddenly come in for careful consideration. If continued shortfalls and price rises appear likely, the switch to substitutes may be on. In many cases, the anxiety of contemplating downtime because of supplier stockouts is worse than the reality, but it still must be dealt with.

One way to counteract a move away from your product is through cost justification. Another is through benefit comparison. A third is to gain access to a substitute material yourself, either by outright acquisition or in a joint venture. In this way, you will always have something to sell. You will also free your salesmen from arguing the merits of your usual products because you will be able to supply competitive materials as well.

These issues may become paramount in many major industries in the next few years. If you think they will affect your accounts, head off the questions before your customers' thinking goes too far. Don't be afraid to bring up the subject for fear of putting ideas into their heads, either. The ideas are probably there already, but your counter-proposals aren't. Even before they ask you the ultimate question, influence their planning with your ultimate answers.

When Being Fully Competitive Means Identically Competitive, You Need More to Sell Than Quality and Price

When you find yourself up to industry standard on quality and price, that's not the end of selling strategy. It's only the beginning of the beginning.

Sales manager: My sales representative tells me he's having a difficult time selling you, so I thought I'd better find out why. Maybe the chemistry between the two of you isn't right. It can't be our product or our prices. No one else can beat us there.

Customer: There's no way you can beat anyone else, either. Your competitors come in here every day and sell the same things you do: quality products, dependable service, and fair prices.

Manager: If we're all selling the same things, then I'd like to ask you for our proper share of your business.

Customer: You're getting it. You think it's an improper share because you'd like it to be larger. Tell me the truth: What you really want is 100%, right?

Manager: What's wrong with that? We could handle it. And you'd benefit. You said yourself that our quality, service, and price are fully competitive.

Customer: They're *identically* competitive, and we want to encourage you to stay that way. It helps keep us from becoming dependent on any single supplier. And it keeps you from becoming too dependent on us as your major customer. You'll have to find another way to sell if you want more of our business; asking for all of it won't work.

Manager: I'd like your help in doing that. What's wrong with the way we're selling you now?

Customer: Your man comes in to see me twice a month to offer me a quality product and professional backup services at a fair price. He calls that *selling* me. He isn't selling me anything at all. Those are just the minimum daily requirements.

Manager: So what does he need to fatten them up, better quality at even cheaper prices? If that's the name of the game here, then I'll throw in the towel right now.

Customer: All we'd get out of that would be to lose you as a supplier. You'd go broke eventually. When I say find another way to sell, I mean sell something over and above quality and price. They're equal to everybody else's. What you need is an inequality to counteract the sameness you have going for you now.

Manager: Where am I going to find an inequality that can do something good for you and still increase our profits?

Customer: Increase ours.

Manager: Increase our profits by increasing yours? How do you see our quality story being tied to that kind of approach?

Customer: I don't, but you can't blame me for that. Your competitors took the edge off your quality story, not I. They equalled your services. I didn't. They matched or undercut your prices. So all of you come in here and promise to increase our profits in much the same way and by almost the same amount: free services that reduce our costs, improved productivity as a result of your product's efficiencies, and so on.

Manager: But that's how we help increase your profit when you buy from us. There's no getting away from that.

Customer: Then how about adding something—how shall I put it—more top-of-the-line?

Manager: Careful, you almost said more expensive. Are you prepared for that?

Customer: Not only prepared: ready and willing, provided that if I end up having to pay more, you end up increasing my profits even more.

Manager: O.K., how's this for starters on your top-of-the-line idea? I'll add two new technical support people to my sales representatives' backup team. They'll be charged with one main responsibility: cutting your losses from assembly downtime and quality control by more than you pay for the service. In other words, they'll be free. In addition, they'll give you the highest rate of production in your industry and as close to zero defects as we can come.

Customer: That sounds all right for starters.

Manager: You could use one of our customer service programs, too, I'll bet. We'll train your people to use properly what you buy from us. That will get you further increases in productivity, prevent costly mistakes, and relieve you of the cost of training those people yourself. That all helps increase profits for you, right?

Customer: It helps.

Manager: How about helping your salespeople learn how to include the chief performance benefits of our products among the selling points they make for your own products? As a matter of fact, why not let us help them sell the same way you and I are talking right now: *Sell to their own customers on the basis of increasing customer profit as a result of dealing with you?*

Customer: That will interest our sales manager. It's intriguing what you've been doing with me. You're beginning to sell me something I can sell internally, you're showing me how I can sell it, and you're making it seem worth buying over and above what we pay for your present products and service package.

Manager: Can you put your finger on the specific sales appeals I itemized that turned you on? I'd like to relay them to my sales force.

Customer: Just one: where you said you could help us increase our profits.

Manager: But I said that about all of them. When you get right down to it, that's all we sell.

Customer: When you get right down to it on our side, that's all we want to buy. Why don't you come back with your sales representative so we *can* get right down to it?

When You're Tied with a Competitor for a Key Account, Make Your Pitch to the Customer's Life Cycle

Talking at the purchasing agent level about your competitors may be all right—the P.A. is paid to listen. But when you go upstairs, the only competitors a customer cares about are his own.

Sales representative: When I came to work here, you told me we were tops in the industry, just like the old Yankees. So how come most of the time I find myself in a tie ball game with competitors that aren't supposed to be able to carry our shoes? The only tiebreaker I have in my kit is to buy my way on base by cutting price.

Field sales manager: That's what happens when you work for an established business. It's the price you pay for selling a leading product made by a reliable house that's invited to bid on any important job. What you're complaining about actually is our strength: We're always in the ball game. It's a tie game for us a lot of the time when someone else would never even have been invited to play.

Representative: But how do we score the winning run? Where do we get the extra strength to do that?

Manager: By understanding the situation, by knowing where you stand in the game so that you know what strategy to use to break the tie. That's the added value that you have to give us over and above our traditional strength, which gets us into the ballpark.

Representative: What do you mean, "knowing where I stand in the game"?

Manager: Let me stretch it out for you. Let's say that this chart represents where product lines of one customer stand in their life cycles. We'll label the newest product A, the biggest winner B, and the longtime market franchiser C. Suppose you're selling to this customer's C product. How can you break a tie situation for us?

Representative: First of all, I have to recognize that the customer is probably very cost-conscious about his C. It's making money for him, but its margins are probably low. This is a typical commodity situation: He's stuck with a low price, so he's extra careful not to add a penny more of cost in buying from us.

Manager: So how do you break the tie?

Representative: There are only two things I can do, other than lower my price. One is to show him how buying from me will reduce his cost the most, say, by using our inventory-control system. The other is to show him how I can help him get added volume so that he can make as much money as possible even with his low margins. How? Possibly by merchandising the benefits of our product to his customers.

Manager: All right. Let's turn our thinking to this same customer's A product. That's the new one that isn't even breaking even yet. How can you break a tie situation here?

Representative: With an A, the cost factor is once again paramount. Only now it's the development and marketing costs that make the customer unwilling to pay our price. He can't afford to add to those costs or he may never reach the breakeven point. So if it's a tie, I have to do one thing better than my competition: show the customer how buying from me can help him either earn more sales on his A or cut his costs.

Manager: Cost is certainly a prime consideration with every customer's new product, but there's another factor, too. What's he most afraid of with an A?

Representative: That it won't ever become a B; that it will stop growing and never reach a payback, let alone a substantial profit.

Manager: What clue does that give you in the tiebreaker department?

Representative: To work more closely with him on his new products than my competitors, to help him grow them and nurse them along, to show concern and be consultative with him.

Manager: That last comment should lead us to strategies for breaking ties that have to do with a customer's B products. What do you suggest?

Representative: The main problem with a B is to prevent it from slipping over the hump of the profit curve and becoming a commodity. I guess my main chance to be a tiebreaker is to help a customer maintain the premium price that sets off the B as a brand. I can try to help him keep it priced above competition for as long as possible, and maybe even raise it.

Manager: And how would you go about doing that?

Representative: By helping the customer make the product the most beneficial on the market. That, obviously, should include selling him our components and the performance advantages they deliver. I would teach him how to promote these advantages to his own customers so that the perceived value of his product would be the highest of all offerings in his category. I would even teach his people how to teach *their* customers how to install, maintain, and use his product to get the full range of our benefits.

Manager: You used the word *teach* a lot just then. How come?

Representative: Because a B product situation is just that: a teaching opportunity for us. Nobody knows enough about how to keep a B from becoming a C. Yet a B is a customer's big profit maker because it can command a premium price and it's above the breakeven point. A customer can use all the help he can get to keep a B winning for him. He can especially use the kind of help I can give him.

Manager: Which is . . .

Representative: Help on knowing more about why his customers buy from him. That's what I call teaching. He can use what I know to make his product zero in on market needs. He can use my knowledge to apply his product better and to advertise it better, which means making it more meaningful to his customers. In fact, the more I think about it, I don't see how he can maintain a B product without me.

Manager: Does that give you insight into what your tiebreaker really is in the most important selling situation for us—the times when we have a true growth opportunity with a customer's high-velocity product?

Representative: Sure. Market smarts—knowing *his* customer's needs. That's my big gun: knowing them and teaching them.

Manager: But we pay you to sell. How do you suggest we finance your second career as a teacher?

Representative: By the added profit I can bring in from my on-the-job teaching. You see, that gives us the right to charge a premium price, too.

Manager: You get an A for that one.

Representative: But I'm really a B because of my premium price.

When a Customer Asks What's New, He May Mean with Him and Not You

The salesperson hasn't been born yet who doesn't want a new product to sell. But the salesperson hasn't been born yet who is selling the full advantages of existing products either.

Sales representative: What's the point of sending us out there every day to sell harder, sell smarter, sell up in customer management, or sell out in breadth, when the truth of the matter is that we have nothing to sell?

Field sales manager: From the looks of our inventory, I'd say we have plenty to sell.

Representative: I mean nothing to sell that's a distinct product advantage: nothing unique, no input from our lab to give us something to crow about.

Manager: The technical people in the lab complain to me that we aren't selling the advantages they've already built into our line. They say it's our fault. Now you're telling me it's theirs. I wish we could direct this internal hostility outward to our competitors.

Representative: How do the technical people know what sells? They live in a cloister. The real world is the buyer interface. That's where I'm being told we're in the me-too business.

Manager: Suppose you could get the lab to turn out a unique advantage, as I think you called it. What would it be?

Representative: I can't tell you what it would *be*. But I can tell you the kinds of things I'd like it to *do*. I'd like a performance advantage, some kind of operating plus that would let me say to a customer, "We're the best. We do the job faster. We keep on the job longer without maintenance. There's less to go wrong. We don't require the labor investment our competitors' products need." Things like that.

Manager: All right, let's assume you could say things like that.

233

How would you sell? Would you just go out into the marketplace, recite your advantages, and then stand back from the customer stampede?

Representative: Of course not. I learned not to sell better mousetraps long ago. I'd have to interpret the advantages into benefits. And I couldn't just throw the product on the customer's desk and send the bill. I'd have to teach him how to apply the benefits and make sure he did it properly.

Manager: So you'd have to do the same kind of interpretive selling, the same applications selling, and the same teaching you're doing right now?

Representative: Sure, but at least I'd have something to interpret and apply.

Manager: Don't you have that now?

Representative: Oh, I can interpret the advantages we have now. That's what I spend my time on. The fewer advantages you have, the longer it takes to try to make something out of them.

Manager: But you told me you're too experienced to sell product advantages—that you sell the end benefits to the user. Not the mousetrap, but freedom from eaten cheese and sweeping up after the mice. I don't understand why our current end-user benefits aren't impressive.

Representative: I think they impress us more than they impress our customers. The main trouble is that they've heard all about our advantages for a long time. They can almost recite them in unison with me as I go down the list. Besides, our competitors have the same list.

Manager: We're not communicating. You keep talking about product advantages. I'm talking about the end values the customer receives from our product advantages. Let me give you an example. If we can reduce a customer's processing time, that's a product advantage. The user's advantage is the dollar value of that saved time. We don't save him time; we save him money. The more money we save him, the more we help him improve his profit. And the more we improve his profit, the more likely he is to buy from us. Isn't that what you should be selling?

Representative: Essentially, that's what I am selling. The problem comes when our competition sells the same thing.

Manager: By the same thing, do you mean a similar product? I grant you that. Do you mean a similar type of advantage, such as lower processing cost? I grant you that, too. But do you also mean that our competitors' sales force is as knowledgeable about customer processes as we are? Are they as adept in creating partnerships with customers as we are, so that hidden cost areas inside customers' processes are equally revealed to them as they are to us? If you say yes to those questions, you're not condemning the lab; you're condemning yourself.

Representative: Maybe we can do those things better than we do now. I can't claim that we're perfect. But new products out of the lab would make it all a lot easier.

Manager: For how long? Only until competition copied our innovation. Then we'd be right back where we are now, selling our own skill in putting our product to work to improve customer profit. Also, any new product will carry a higher price. That means you would have to sell our applications skill harder to deliver added value to justify the added cost. And don't overlook the added education you'd have to give the customer on any new product. Don't think I'm knocking new products. I'm not. I'm knocking an attitude that says we can't sell without them.

Representative: So what you're saying is that value-adding opportunities are available now in our customer's business that we can get at with our present products. And that even with new products, the problem would be exactly the same: Sell the applications advantages, not the product advantages.

Manager: You said that so well that I'm going to give you a reward. How would you like to offer your customers a brand-new product tomorrow morning?

Representative: What kind?

Manager: Your renewed dedication to working with our present product line to improve their profit better than anyone has ever done before.

Becoming the Market Leader Becomes Possible Once You Make Your Customers the Leaders in Their Own Markets

"Leadership," the sales manager says, "That's what we're known for in our industry. We get the business because people know we're the best."

"The best in what?" I ask.

"That's a good question," he answered. "It depends. Last year we led the industry in sales, but we paid such a high price for them that our profits fell out of bed. Up to a few years ago, we were the acknowledged price leader. Now we wheel and deal with the best of them.

"We still lead in quality, though. But unfortunately, we put so much into our products that there's no way we can claim leadership as the low-cost producer. I guess leadership is a complicated business. How do you define it?"

"I generally use a single standard. I say that the leader in an industry is the company that helps its customers the most."

"Oh," says the manager, "a customer-oriented definition of leadership. So what do you do, run around and ask all the customers in an industry who helps them the most before you can identify the leader?"

"That's one way. But there's another. A leadership company sells in a distinctive style that's based on five characteristics. If you look for those characteristics, you can generally pick out the leader even without knowing very much about his markets."

To pursue the matter, I ask the man what his company sells.

"We sell product performance at a price," he says.

"Well, that's not what a leader sells. *The prime benefit a leader sells*

236

is his ability to improve his customer's profit or reduce his costs. That's the first characteristic of a leader: In one way or another, he promises to have a favorable effect on his customer's financial process."

"O.K. The leading supplier sells the best benefit. But improving a customer's profit is a service; what if you're a product company?"

"Whether its a product or a service supplier, a leadership company defines its business in terms of delivering a service that affects a customer's bottom line. Leaders always promote themselves as service organizations."

"What about their products?" the manager asks.

"They position their products as the means, *not the* end; that's the second characteristic of leadership. Merchandise becomes simply a vehicle for profit improvement, which, as you say, is a service."

"If you push not the products, but their ability to deliver a service benefit, how do you talk to customers?"

"*You talk to them about their business,*" I say, "*not yours.* That's the third characteristic. Don't go around proclaiming how well you know your own processes or how good your own products are. Make it clear to the customer that you know his business and that's why you can help him improve his profit."

"But doesn't that suggest that you know a customer's business better than he does? In the first place, how can that be possible? And secondly, even if it's true, isn't it heresy to say it?"

"This takes a little tact, to be sure. But, realistically, if you're the leader, you know more than your customer about the areas of his business that you affect because you work with many companies. You bring him experience he can get only through you."

"I still don't see," the sales manager interrupts, "how you can dare say that."

"I don't see how you can dare *not* say it if it's accurate," I say. "Remember our definition of leadership: helping your customers the most. How can you help them unless you share your experience and expertise with them? That doesn't mean you tell a customer how to run his business. All you're saying is that he can run it more profitably with your help than without it."

"If talking about your knowledge of a customer's business is the third characteristic of a leader, what does that do to your advertising and your sales promotion?"

"Ideally, promotion is used to prove your claims of being able to deliver improved profit. You promote case histories of how your customers succeeded as a result of your help. Your whole approach is, 'Look what *they* did.' "

The sales manager reflects for a moment. "So if I want to be the leader, I have to throw away everything our sales force uses that says we are the best in the business in this or that, or we were the first to discover or invent such and such. Is that what you're suggesting?"

"Unless you want someone else to take the ball away from you by saying, 'Our *customers* are the best in *their* business, with our help.' "

"All right. So what's the fourth characteristic of a market leader?"

"The salesman for a leading company teaches his customers a how-to approach. He consults with them on how they can obtain the benefits he is uniquely qualified to provide. When he does that teaching job well, he creates a strong partnership with his customers. They learn that together they can accomplish what neither of them can do alone: improve profits for both their companies. In that sense, the leader converts his customer into a client. *All leaders have consultant-client relationships with their customers.*"

"So what's the fifth characteristic?" the manager asks. "I suppose it's something like, 'The leader is always loved.' "

"Just the opposite. Leaders are respected, needed, envied, and imitated, yes. But loved? I don't think so. In fact, you could say that the fifth characteristic of leadership is that *the leader's customers are often defensive about doing business with him.*

"That's not because he isn't good for them; it's because he's generally the high-priced supplier. Customers may have to justify doing business with the most expensive source when other options are available."

"If that's true, when I ask a customer who does business with a leader why he pays a premium price to do so, what answer should I get—'Because I want the best'?"

"No. A very defensive answer: 'Because I *had to.*' The leader's customer should feel he really has no choice. Only the leader knows enough about improving the profit in his kind of business. If he can deliver on that promise, price is secondary."

"Your characteristics of leadership sound simple enough. Why can't salesmen for any company claim them?"

"They can."

"What if they deliver?"

"Then they've made *their company* the leader."

If You Have a Satisfied Customer on Your Hands, You May Have No Customer at All

The sales manager glares at his troops. "Clarity of purpose!" he shouts. "Sense of mission!" Without them, we're just ragtag and bobtail. What good does it do to get up every morning and go out there to sell if we don't know why we're doing it?"

He fixes their eyes for a full minute and then goes on. "Here's an assignment for each of you. On page 1 of your new sales plan for the coming year, I want you to write your statement of mission. No more than one sentence; 25 words, even less. Write down what's going to guide you to the volume you're committed to. I'll give you a hint of what I'd like to see: I want you to maximize sales. And I want you to satisfy your customers."

One of the salespeople raises his hand. "No offense," he says, "but those two objectives are totally incompatible."

Mission statements used to be the sole province of top management's strategic plans. They gave "loft" to the enterprise, containing such worthy goals as quality, value, and good corporate citizenship. Lately, it's become fashionable to work the mission concept down to the sales level. Many managers are latching onto the idea, convinced that having objectives will help. They also figure that stating objectives may provide a sense of direction to what can otherwise be an opportunistic frenzy to make quota.

"Incompatible?" the manager asks. "How could you possibly have the first without the second?"

"The way I look at it," the man answers, "I don't see how you can ever have the first if you do have the second." One look at the manager tells him that he'd better explain. "All the really important sales I've ever made have come from *dissatisfied* customers. Some of them were dissatisfied with their present suppliers, but those were the minority. The ones I've done the best with are customers who are dissatisfied with the way something is going in their businesses. They're searching for greater satisfaction and I try to help them."

"Give me a 'for-instance.' " the manager says.

"Take a customer whose inventory turnover is lower than the industry average," says the salesperson. "He's dissatisfied because he knows that it affects his profits, but he doesn't know what to do about it, or even whether it's possible to do anything at all. He's the kind of customer I want.

"Or take a customer whose collection of receivables is lagging. He's dissatisfied with his cash flow. I want him, too. And along with him, I want customers who are dissatisfied with their quality control, their productivity—anything I can help with. The more dissatisfied they are, the better prospects they make."

"So once you find them and classify them as dissatisfied, you satisfy them. Is that it?" the manager asks.

"Oh, no. I try to make them just a little bit *less* dissatisfied by the help I provide. I call it 'incremental relief.' I take the pressure off them in stages, little by little. I want their dissatisfaction quotient to come down gradually as we work together. But I never want them to be satisfied."

"Why not? If you're going to maximize your sales opportunity with them," the manager says, "you've got to satisfy them at some point."

"A dissatisfied customer is a buying customer," the salesperson explains. "Once a customer reaches satisfaction, he'll stop focussing on whatever it is and concentrate his dissatisfaction—and dollars— somewhere else. Satisfaction is stasis. I want the customer who is in dynamic equilibrium, doing something with me today and, based on the improvement we achieve, doing something more with me tomorrow and beyond."

"That means you deliberately keep your customers dissatisfied?" the manager wants to know.

"No, that's not it. I deliberately channel their dissatisfaction into constructive solutions. But nothing in an ongoing business is ever solved once and for all. How can a customer be totally satisfied? If something in his business is off-spec today, he wants to make it better. By tomorrow, however, someone may have set a new standard, so he'll want to make it better still. If he becomes complacent and rests on his laurels, the race may pass him by. The reason he needs me is to make sure that he doesn't settle for last year's averages to win this year's ball game."

"But isn't there some point," the manager persists, "when you want a satisfied customer? How about referral time, when someone else in the industry calls him and asks whether his relationship with us is satisfactory? How do you handle that?"

The salesperson says, "I brief my customers about that in advance. I tell them that they can evaluate our relationship at any given time in one simple way: by comparing their costs and productivity after working with me with what they were before. Are they improved? Are they continuing to trend toward further improvement? I want yes answers to those questions. Then I ask them whether they're satisfied to stop here. That's where I want a no, because that's where my next order comes from."

"And what do your prospects say when they get a reference on you like that?" the manager asks.

"They usually tell me they're dissatisfied with the same problems that are bothering my customers. They want to know whether I can help them, too. Some of them go a little further. They tell me they're even dissatisfied with the improvements I've been getting for my customers, and they want to challenge me to see whether I can get even more profit increases for them."

"What do you tell them?"

"I tell them I find that quite satisfactory."

If You're Tired
of Competing Against the
Same Old Vendors, Try
Competing Against Your
Customers

"What do you mean, you have a new competitor for me?" the sales representative, horrified, asks his manager, "I don't need any more competitors. Send me more customers."

"You're in luck this time," the manager says. "This one's both."

This strange dialogue goes on in more and more sales forces these days. The reason is simple. If you make rival suppliers your competitors, the customer is forced to make comparisons between your performances. If they are equal, or close enough to parity not to matter, the only comparison where meaningful differences can occur is price. Supplier-vs.-supplier competition is almost always price competition.

But what happens when the customer is regarded as your competitor? Now a true performance distinction can generally be made: the difference between what it costs the customer right now to maintain a problem in his operations and the reduced cost you can help him achieve. When this difference is significant, as it often is, and you are the first to discover it and propose a solution, your price will be irrelevant.

"Irrelevant?" the sales representative asks, astonished. "How can price be irrelevant? Do you mean I can charge any price I want to and there won't be any resistance?"

"No, not any price," the manager says. "But any price that has a fair relation to the value of the customer's costs you reduce. And that price will always be higher than you can charge when you go head to head with another supplier."

"What you're saying, then," the representative says to his manager, who is nodding agreement, "is that if I make price the only relevant decision, the customer will naturally buy on it. If I make adding value the relevant decision—how much I can add compared to how much the customer is able to add by himself—the customer will buy the added value as long as the price. . . . What's the rest of the sentence?"

"As long as the price still gives the customer a fair return. In other words, as long as the value you add exceeds its cost."

Competing against a customer's capability in running many of his cost-burdened operations should be easy. After all, that's what being a problem-solving supplier is all about. A customer runs many functions in his business. You specialize in one or perhaps a few. It stands to reason that you should know more about reducing their cost; that is the reward for your experience. Many functions in a customer's business have nothing to do with the main skills of his expertise. Why, for example, should a brewer whose prime skill is in brewing beer be an expert in all the aspects of its distribution? Why should an energy company be expert in telecommunications? If you are the expert, this is your market.

"I see a catch," the representative says. "How many purchasing agents will understand me when I try to learn their company's costs so I can reduce them? How many of them will understand my pricing if I base it on the value of reducing those costs? 'Respond to the request for proposal,' they'll tell me. 'Give me a regular bid.' "

"Why shouldn't they?" the manager asks. "How many years have you been teaching them how to do business with you that way? What you're telling me is that they've learned. O.K., since you're such a good teacher and they're such good learners, teach them the new way."

"Suppose they're comfortable the way they are? Suppose they say no thanks?"

"Some of them are bound to, but not all of them will. All you need is one to start with."

"Suppose one says yes. Then what do I do?"

"What do *we* do," corrects the manager. "The two of you go upstairs in the customer's organization and find managers of processes whose costs you can reduce. You learn what the costs amount to, from the managers and from any other reliable source you can find in the company. Then you come back to me and we work out a proposal to bring them down at a price that represents a premium buy for the customer and a premium profit for ourselves."

"What if we do all this," the representative asks, "and the customer says, 'Thanks a lot; now I'm going to send your proposal out to bid?' Now we're right back where we started with price as the main factor. What then?"

"Some customers may do that. But most won't. We'll show them how costly it is to delay getting the cost savings we can provide; how even if they get a lower price they will have deprived themselves of added profits while they're out for bids. Time is money, and we'll prove to them how much."

"You make the customer seem like a very desirable competitor," the representative says, elated. "I'd better get busy. For the first time in my life, I can be honest in saying that it would be a crying shame if we lost a competitor."

Make Your Customer Comfortable with Being Surprised, and He Won't Make You Uncomfortable by Surprising You

"When I started out in selling," the representative tells his sales manager, "one of the first rules I was taught was to make the customer comfortable. Give him what he expects. Be dependable. Make reliability your middle name. And no surprises. Now you tell me that, to be a proper partner with my customer, I've got to learn how to use surprise. I don't get it."

"You're looking at it as an either-or," the manager says. "That's why you aren't getting it. The secret is how you *combine* the two. Comfort without surprise leads to complacency. Surprise without comfort is anarchy."

More than ever before, sales relationships are up for grabs. Even long-standing personal relationships are at risk. Purchasers are limiting the number of sales representatives who call on them. It is no longer sufficient to meet specifications or to be a "loyal supplier." On one hand, buyers are saying, "If you're not a major source of supply for us, we can't take the time to see you." On the other, suppliers are restricting their calls. If a customer isn't a key account, he may never see the representatives of many suppliers. They will do business with him by mail or telemarketing.

"Comfort," the manager says, "is based on meeting expectations. The most important expectation we can meet is to be important to the customer, to meet his expectation that we do something important for him. Otherwise, why will he see us? Thus our first order of business is to determine which we are going to do for a customer so that he can come to count on us being advantageous to him. In your case, what would you say that is?"

"I improve the profits of my customers," the representative answers. "That's what I tell my key accounts they can count on when they do business with me."

"Do you prove that to them?"

"Right up front, even before we do business for the first time. That's how I spend most of my development time with a customer. It's not a question of proving that our product works, or even that it works better than our competitors'. It is proving to him that I'm going to add new profits to his bottom line."

"Does that make him comfortable?" asks the manager.

"Better than anything else I've ever sold. Once he lets me prove it and he sees how much I can cut his costs or help him raise his sales, he finds it very comfortable to work with me this way. That is why I can't understand why you want me to surprise him about anything!"

"In a perfect world," the manager says, "you and your customers would be partners for life. You would go in improving their profits year after year. They would go on rewarding you with more and more business at premium prices. But, unfortunately, we do not live in a perfect world. What kinds of things do you think about that could disturb your comfort level with an account?"

"The person I have cultivated at a customer company—he's practically my partner—could be promoted to another job where he would no longer be involved with me. Or he could take early retirement. In other words, I could lose him."

"How else could you lose him?"

"One of our competitors could take him away from me, replace me as his partner."

"On what basis could that occur?" the manager asks.

"One of them could offer him something that I'm not making available, I guess. I can't think of any other reason."

"Would that surprise you?"

"I'll say—oh, now I get it," the representative says. "You want me to surprise him first, before a competitor surprises both of us by doing something for him that we're not."

When a supplier is actively involved in serving a customer, it is difficult to see what *may not* be happening, opportunities that are going undetected or problems that remain unsolved. Yet, to a competitor seeking to unseat a supplier, these are often the first openings he sees. How surprising would it be, we must ask ourselves, if a competitor were to pick up on one of these opportunities and make an inroad into our prized relationship? If it would surprise us, it would probably surprise our customer as well. How come, he could very well ask us, we never offered to help him in that area of his business? What kind of partner are we?

"So what should I look for in the way of surprises?" the representative wants to know.

"First of all," the manager counsels, "think like the customer. What is his hidden agenda? What would he like to accomplish that isn't on his present list? Can we help him? If you think so, surprise the customer.

"Second, think like a competitor. What openings are we leaving for him? Where can he outflank us, make an end run around us, catch us unprotected or off guard? Should we be doing those things ourselves? If you think so, surprise the customer in a different way."

"If I act that way with my key customers," the representative says, "then won't I be making them comfortable again—comfortable with me as someone who keeps surprising them with unexpected ways of improving their profits? In addition to all the expected things I'm already doing, I mean?"

"I'd be surprised if that weren't the case," the manager says. "In fact, I could get really comfortable with the idea."

There's No Mystery to Sales Force Productivity—Just Make the Customer More Productive

Sales force productivity is much more than having more time to stand before the customer. It's delivering more satisfaction when you do, so that the customer will invite you back to do it again.

Field sales manager: Have you seen the latest *Sales and Marketing Management* figures on the cost of a sales call? You may be surprised to hear that for as many as 20% of your sales the cost is unaffordable.

Sales representative: Why's that?

Manager: Those sales don't bring us enough profit to break even, let alone earn anything. That means one thing to me: Your productivity isn't meeting our new standards.

Representative: What are they?

Manager: From now on, every one of our reps must contribute profit at an annual rate of 10 times his cost. And your cost includes not just salary and fringes but also the cost of your calls. If 20% or more of them are unprofitable, you won't make it.

Representative: At that level I'm not being "productive?"

Manager: Not productive enough to stay with us, no matter how many sales you make.

Representative: But I've been following the system you've set up: Make more calls, and sales will increase proportionally. Right?

Manager: Wrong. You're leaving out the key word. Make more *profitable* sales calls. Even then, be selective. Make only the *most* profitable calls.

Representative: How do I know in advance which are most profitable? You don't give me profit figures on my products.

Manager: You don't need them. You know what our big winners are. They're the ones I tell you to push hardest. But from now on I'll make sure you know our profit makers, even if you don't know the exact dollar amount of their contribution.

Representative: I know enough about the business to figure them out pretty closely anyway. Are they the only ones you want me to sell?

Manager: They're the ones I want you to "push-sell." Anything else that you move will be by "pull-sell," where the customer pulls it out of you and really does the selling himself. Those sales should be zero-time, zero-effort deliveries for you.

Representative: But aren't these other products—the "little-winners"—important to us?

Manager: Sure they are. We like the incremental revenues they add. But they're profitable only if we don't have to invest much time and effort to sell them.

Representative: But a lot of our customers want them. How do we deal with that?

Manager: Oh, we'll still sell them. But *we* will, not you. You're too valuable to us, too expensive. We'll sell our lower-profit items by telephone or mail. We may even use distributors, outside reps, or other volume movers.

Representative: So you're leaving me with the high-ticket lines: more profiitable to us but more expensive for our customers.

Manager: Not "but"—*therefore* more expensive to buy. That's why they're profitable.

Representative: Doesn't that make my life more difficult? I've got the toughest products from the point of view of price. Competition will walk all over me. If I call you and ask for price relief, you won't give me any because, if you do, we won't have any big winners left to sell. Right?

Manager: Right. But you're overlooking something. How does a big winner get to be a winner in the first place? Who gives it that status?

Representative: The customer, of course. He makes it a best-seller because he finds value in it.

Manager: And doesn't that superior value merit a superior price?

Representative: Not when competition undercuts it. What do I do then?

Manager: Stop selling the product.

Representative: You mean throw it out of the line?

Manager: No. I mean stop selling the product and start selling the customer. If the product's performance values won't bring you a highly profitable price, sell the values the product can add to the customer's business.

Representative: First you take away the easy sellers and leave me only the big winners. Now you take them away, too, and say that my productivity depends on adding values to the customer's business. Isn't that what the product is for?

Manager: Only partly. Mostly, that's what *you* are for. The way you add to your productivity is to add to the customer's productivity.

Representative: By selling the product.

Manager: By solving customer problems that require use of our product. No product can perform for a customer unless it's applied. No sales rep can be productive at today's selling costs unless he's a professional in applications. To be that, and to apply his product, he's got to know the customer's problems.

Representative: So what you're really telling me is not to forget about volume, but go after a new kind: big-volume sales of big-ticket products to big-problem customers.

Manager: For whom you have the big profit-improvement solution. Remember, if you don't help customers apply our big winners to improve their profit, they won't buy enough from us to help increase your own profits.

Representative: It seems to me that if I concentrate my selling this way—stop chasing smokestacks and settle down to solve customers' problems—I could conceivably raise the cost of my sales even higher than it is now. What would happen then?

Manager: You can raise it as high as you want. Just be sure you raise your profitable sales volume even higher so that your productivity meets our new standards. I won't evaluate you on cost alone. What I'm interested in is what I get for the cost.

Representative: Say, what kind of reasoning led you to these new standards anyway: inductive or deductive?

Manager: Productive.

Sell the Customer First—Then It's a Lot Easier to Sell the Product

All customers want to be satisfied with the products they buy. But even more important, they want to be satisfied with their businesses as a result.

Sales representative: My customer won't switch. I suspected it from the beginning—now I'm sure of it. How many more times do you want me to prove the same thing over and over again to myself?

Sales manager: Until you've proved it to me. That means at least one more time. I'm willing to believe you've been selling the product. But you obviously haven't sold the customer. Remember: Until you sell the customer you'll never sell the product. Take the customer's point of view with me. Role-play the customer's perspective of your relationship. What would it sound like in his own words?

Representative: I think he has respect for me. I don't have any trouble getting in to see him. I think he'd say I know my product, that I represent it fairly so that he can trust me, that I'm maybe a cut or two above the other vendors he sees, and that my price is on the high side of fair. Did I say all the right things?

Manager: I don't know. I wasn't listening to what you said. I was listening for what you didn't say.

Representative: What didn't I say?

Manager: You didn't say that he was the one who wanted to see you—just that you didn't have trouble seeing him. You didn't say he thought you knew his business—just that you knew your own product. You didn't say he perceived you as someone very different from your competitors—just that you are maybe a cut or two above them.

Representative: But why should he be the one who wants to see me? After all, I'm selling.

Manager: That's probably the problem right there. Next time you call on him, don't sell. Give something away—no, not the product. What? There are various answers to this question. They all add up to information: facts about the customer's business, about his market, and about his products, all in the areas of performance where our products affect them. Give knowledge about the customer's business, not our own, except insofar as we can influence it for the better.

Representative: But how do I learn about his business and how ours relates to it?

Manager: Two ways. First, get inside his business. Get to see the people whose operations are involved with what we sell. Learn their problems and opportunities. Come back then and get to see our own people. Learn from them how we can solve those problems. Then go back to the customer and teach what you've learned.

Representative: Suppose he already knows the problems.

Manager: All the better. That way, he knows that they're real and that they're unsolved. He may even be so interested in what your approach to a solution will be that he will actively want to see you.

Representative: What if he'll talk to me about the problems but he won't let me get inside his business to see his people all by myself?

Manager: Invite him to come along with you so he can know what you're doing—even make his own contribution to it. If he won't go along, ask him to make your appointments for you so that he can keep control of your comings and goings. Report back to him after every meeting.

Representative: It might be even worse than that. Maybe he won't let me in under any circumstances. How should I react if he wants to take my information and solution and present them himself?

Manager: Offer to go along with him as a silent support resource just in case you're needed. If he doesn't pick up on that, offer to sit in his office to be available on the phone if he needs your help. If he won't go for that either, offer to have a coaching session with him before he goes.

Representative: What am I trying to do by all this, make the customer my agent or my salesman or what?

Manager: The correct answer is neither of the above. The

answer is to make the customer our *partner,* someone who has something in common with us so that both of us can act in the same interest. Is it that we want the customer to sell for us, then? No. We want the customer to sell for him and for his company in the role of our inside partner. Why will he do this? Only because his own self-interest has been aroused by what we can do to help him and he wants to participate with us in the reward.

Representative: So should I tell him I want to be his partner instead of someone who wants to sell him something?

Manager: Don't tell him that in words. Tell him by the way you act.

Representative: But I'm afraid I won't be a good partner when I start. I've never done it before.

Manager: Probably neither has he. Certainly not with you. So here's a chance for both of you to learn how to be partners together. But don't forget that the initiative has to come from you. Selling a customer on becoming a partner with us is far more difficult then selling a product. But unless we do, we may never be able to sell. The reason is simple. It takes two to make a sale.

Representative: So now that we've learned something about our business together, I'd better get going and sell . . .

Manager and representative (together): Someone!

8
Sales
Management

Taking Charge of the 20% of Things That Give 80% of the Results

To Increase Profits, Play Santa Claus: Give Everybody 24 Free Hours a Month

"Our profit per average sale is declining," the manager tells his key account sales force. "That means one thing to me: You people aren't managing your businesses. You're not selling our high-margin lines, not concentrating on making sales that are the biggest profit makers for us. Why?"

The answers are easy—and the same in company after company. Let the sales representatives say it for themselves:

• "Our high-margin lines are high-priced. We get too much customer resistance. It takes too long to sell."

• "Our reward system, which is what you evaluate us on, pays off in volume, not profit. I sell anything I can to make my units."

The amount of profit per average sale is becoming an increasingly important index as quarterly reports increasingly show that sales are up but earnings are down. The sales function is coming under scrutiny by top managers. They see it this way: Costs are up, but the return on each additional dollar invested is down. The relationship between volume and profit is seen more clearly, and often this comes as a shock.

Under pressure from the top to shape up their forces (especially those who call on key accounts, where the profit contribution from sales is greatest) before they ship them out, managers are haunted by the problem of what-are-my-people-doing-out-there. One manager I know has an unusual approach to this problem. He starts by telling the troops:

"You say you sell whatever moves quickly because we reward you for volume. You sell what the customer tells you he needs instead of taking the time to make a detailed needs analysis so that *you* can tell *him*. You say you back off from price resistance. All right, I'll tell you what I'm going to do.

"I'm going to give every one of you a gift. But be careful, this one bites. Each month I'll start you off with a day's worth of man-hours, 24 of them, that are absolutely free. On the basis of your past performance in productivity per man-hour, I'll calculate the sales volume you'd normally generate in 24 hours and deduct it from your monthly quota. Now you can't say I've never done anything nice for you."

Of course there's a catch. How are those 24 man-hours to be spent? Here's what the manager proposes.

"The 24 man-hours I'm freeing up for each of you are to be used for one purpose and only one. Think of them as your investment fund for developing high-profit sales. You say you don't have time? Now you have time. Time to do what? Here's how I'm going to evaluate how much you respect my gift.

"The main thing I'm looking for is new profit dollars from high-volume sales that you would not otherwise have made. That means you have to use those hours to earn more for me than they are currently earning. In fact, these hours must be the most profitable you spend. I'll take three main factors into consideration:

• "Do the sales you make during these 24 hours bring me real profit growth—that is, new profit dollars that are above average on each sale?

• "Are you generating what I call *real proposal growth*? Do you put into your customer's hands new proposals for our high-profit lines at a rate greater than before? Since you all know that our hit ratio is directly proportional to our proposal rate, it's obvious how important this second criterion is.

• "Do you develop real information growth? This means data on your customer's problems and how we can help solve them, new data on your customer's opportunities and how we can help him reach out and achieve them. Do you put this knowledge into your database so that you can use it? Do you use it to crank out more high-margin proposals that will give us above-average profit?"

Underlying this approach to improving profit per average sale is a traditional research principle: investment in negative (up-front) lead time. That's the technical term for the necessary drain on money while development of any kind takes place. Does the sales manager have a strategy for encouraging, if not guaranteeing, a return on his investment of 24 hours of development time for every key account representative each month? You bet he does. He continues:

"Let's put the final piece into place: your incentive. First, the good news. If all that you bring back every 90-day measurement period is the same profit on sales you have been earning on a regular basis, you will be breaking even. No loss, but no gain. However, there is at least the promise of future gain, so I'll go along with you for a few more reporting periods.

"If you exceed your norms, though, I'll share the reward with you at the rate of a dime for every new profit dollar you bring in, up to twice your present average. Surpass twice your average, and I'll double the ante.

"Now the bad news. If you come out below your average, you pay me the difference out of your regular commissions."

When is an incentive an incentive? When it works. This incentive works because it gets to the heart of both the manager's self-interest and the perceptions of key account salespeople as to what constitutes proper reward for risk. Key account productivity, the most important category of results in every sales force, is given its best chance to improve dramatically.

A third party benefits, also: the customer. He buys more high-margin products and services, to be sure, but he receives unusual value from his investments. They are being put to work in his business by a sales representative who is studying the situation in depth and working hard to make it more profitable as well.

Where Do You Need to Allocate Your Sales Force—to Your Rolls-Royces, to Your Hula Hoops, or In Between?

A sales manager is calling on two of his mainstay accounts. Let's eavesdrop on the punch lines of his conversations. Here he is with the first customer:

"You've been a valued customer of ours for more than five years. I'm going to assume that you've valued us as a source of supply all these years as well. We want to maintain those values on both sides. They're being threatened by rising costs, costs that make it unprofitable for us to serve you the way we have and that, in your own business, probably are making it less and less cost-effective for you to deal with us the way you do. I want to propose a solution to keep us both in the business of providing important values to each other.

"We've gone over the records of your transactions with us for the five years of our relationship. Virtually everything you've bought has been on a regular basis. We'd like you to go on doing the same with us. From now on, though, we're going to ask you to do it over a computer terminal instead of with our sales representative."

Now, let's listen in on the second call:

"We've made an audit of the functions that Charlie, our sales representative, has been performing with you for the past 12 months. We've found that almost 80% of them are sales-related but don't involve much selling; things such as order entry, inventory control, and collections. This is all downtime for Charlie as a salesman.

"When we add in the cost of each call for him to perform these functions and match the opportunity cost of his downtime—when

260

he could be selling somewhere else—plus his calling cost with the profit contributed by his sales to you, it's a losing proposition. So we're going to automate all of Charlie's nonselling functions and give Charlie a chance to be more profitable to you and to us. If he can't make it, then we'll automate his selling role as well with a combination of telephone marketing, mail, and electronic communications."

There is a common denominator in these two cases. No, it is not cost, although that is certainly a major determinant. The truly critical common factor is that the sales manager's products were *selling themselves* to both customers. There was no need for a salesperson to be assigned to either of them.

What kinds of products sell themselves? There are two types. One is at the extreme upper end of the positioning scale. These are the Rolls-Royces of an industry that are bought, not sold. You can have a Rolls-Royce product by virtue of its unrivalled technical excellence or market imagery. Either way, a sales representative becomes a mere order taker—an unnecessary added cost.

The other type of product that sells itself is at the low end of the positioning scale. It is the commodity product, the standardized, regularized, homogenized me-too product that competes only on price and availability because its benefits and features have long been replicated by competition. For a product like this, a sales representative again becomes an order taker—in other words, an unnecessary added cost to such products as semiconductors and polypropylene.

Thus we have a remarkable sameness at the two extreme ends of the positioning scale. Neither the Rolls-Royce nor the basic commodity require salespeople, and for the same reason: they sell themselves.

There is, however, one major difference. The cost of a Rolls-Royce sales representative is amply covered by the product's margin. The commodity salesperson's cost is not. In many cases, it contributes the *coup de grace* to profit.

If you have the equivalent of a Rolls-Royce in your product line, examine it to see whether it could sell itself. Even more to the point, see whether it is *already* selling itself. If it is, consider taking your salespeople away from it and reallocating them. At the same time, examine your mature commodity product lines. How many of them are selling themselves? How many more could do so? Take your salespeople away from these products, too, and reallocate them.

What will happen when you do these things that can affect as many as 80% of the products in a large business? You will probably lose some volume—not profit, mind you, but volume. Judging from the experiences of companies that are changing the management of their sales forces in these ways, the loss of volume is small, occurs quickly, and then stabilizes. But because costs drop immediately and significantly, profits rise a great deal more on the slightly reduced volume than they could ever have been boosted by "selling harder" or "selling smarter."

What do you do with the customers in between the Rolls-Royce segment and the commodity buyers who base their decisions on price? These accounts become the target accounts for direct, in-person selling. It is in this area of your business that nothing sells itself. Here, the sales representative can—and should—make the crucial difference. Through his skills, you should be able to command a premium price and thereby earn premium profits. This is the one fertile area for personal selling. But this will be true only if the sales force is trained to sell here.

Selling in this fiercely competitive arena below the Rolls-Royce segment and above the commodity markets demands adherence to a set of five basic principles:

1. Sales must be based on value, not price.
2. Sales must be directed upward to the highest relevant level of customer management, not purchasing.
3. Sales must be made in a consultative manner based not on the representative's product knowledge but on his knowledge of the customer's business.
4. Sales must bring customers demonstrable new profits, not products.
5. Sales presence must be maintained continuously, not sporadically.

Will customers feel deprived when you reallocate your salespeople? Not if you put them to work in each customer's business where they can improve his profits, and yours, even more than before. Will competitors steal your business? Only the business you cannot serve profitably anyway. What will happen to sales force morale? It will rise, because of new earnings per salesperson and an end to wasteful, boring time-serving schedules.

If you don't move in this direction, will a competitor? Undoubtedly.

If You Have an Astonishing Competitor, Devote Yourself to Making Him Incredible

Having competitors is as inevitable as death and taxes. But how we position them is up to us.

Sales representative: All our customers tell me the same story: We're the best presenters. But the business goes to somebody else. We need help.

Field sales manager: What do you suggest?

Representative: I thought that was your job. All right, I'll tell you. We need a top-to-bottom housecleaning of everything we're doing, from the product on down.

Manager: Do you think our product is noncompetitive?

Representative: It's not something that sells itself, that's for sure. O.K., maybe it's not noncompetitive, but's it's no different from anybody else's.

Manager: That means that nobody else's product is any different from ours. Yet you're saying that our competitors are selling undifferentiated products and we're not. Maybe we'd better look elsewhere.

Representative: We don't have to look very far. Look at our promotional material. It says the same things our competitors say. Their material is no different from ours, yet they're selling and we're not. So let's look at price.

Manager: What about price? I don't think you're going to tell me our price is the same as the competition's, are you?

Representative: That's just the point. We have a parity product, standard promotional support, but the highest price in the industry. What kind of sense does that make?

Manager: It makes good sense if we market it properly. The

264

message I'm getting from you is that we're not. I'm going to take a point of view: The problem isn't with our product or promotion or price. It's that we're failing to give our competitors the proper opportunity.

Representative: You've got to be kidding. That's *all* we've been giving them.

Manager: But not the *proper* opportunity. By that I mean the opportunity to be incredible.

Representative: They're already incredible the way they're killing us.

Manager: I'd better explain what I mean. There are two ways I want you to begin making our competitors incredible. The first has to do with price. What can you do to make our competitors price themselves incredibly?

Representative: If they priced higher than we do, that would be unbelievable.

Manager: What about the opposite?

Representative: That's what they're doing now, and none of our customers find it incredible.

Manager: Because we're not helping them to see it that way. We provide standard industry quality, right? It meets all specifications. We're known for our quality control. We've never had a product recall, and nobody's ever sued us for failure to perform. Therefore, our higher price is a natural accompaniment to our quality.

Representative: But our customers will always want to know why our price is higher.

Manager: Why don't you turn the tables on them? Why not ask your customers how competitors' prices can be lower? After all, our costs aren't that much above the rest.

Representative: You mean make our competitors' prices seem *incredibly low* for the kind of quality we perceive as standard?

Manager: Nicely put. So let's say our Rule 1 will be to make our competitors' lower prices appear to be incredibly low in terms of the value they claim to give.

Representative: If that's Rule 1, what's Rule 2?

Manager: Rule 2 has to do with the value our competitors promise. How can we make that aspect of their selling incredible?

Representative: By making them claim even greater value than they can deliver, or than the customer can believe.

Manager: Right. In the case of Rule 1, we make incredible mean incredibly low. In Rule 2, we make it mean incredibly high.

Representative: So you're telling me it's our approach that's at fault. What do you call that theory?

Manager: It's the theory of positioning: how we position our competitors. We've been looking at them as aggressive merchandisers. They've been selling high-perceived quality at low price, and we've allowed ourselves to be positioned in the defensive against their initiative. I'm suggesting we turn it around.

Representative: If we did, how would it come out? We take the offensive and stop apologizing for our high price. Instead of defending the high price we charge for the same quality, we promote price as being justified by standard value. *We become the standard.* Then the low-priced suppliers are thrown on the defensive: how come they can promise equal quality—even superior quality, as one of them likes to imply—at a price below the index of standard quality? Is that the approach?

Manager: Sounds good. Now, how do you think our competitors will respond?

Representative: Let's look at their options. (1) Raise their price? Then they're equal to us. (2) Improve their quality or improve the ways they demonstrate it? That raises their costs and lowers their profits; besides, then they're playing our game. (3) Equal price and equal quality: That puts the premium on the sales force.

Manager: And what would you think of our becoming competitive on those terms?

Representative: Incredible.

When Competition Scares You, Start with the Worst Case and Work Your Way Down

Most salesmen move into management with a simple working definition of a competitor: anyone who can hurt you. Once into a regional or district leadership position, however, many managers quickly realize that all competitors are not created equal. In most multicompany industries, only one or two competitors are capable of inflicting real pain. That scales down the problem to something that can be coped with.

Some sales managers refine their competitive situation even further. They face up to it by starting with the worst case and planning their strategies from that point out.

"When I first took over my territory," one regional manager says, "I used to spend a lot of time beating my head against what I came to think of as the "terrible triangle." I wondered what my competitors would do next, when they might do it, and what effect it would have on my position with key accounts. They one day I decided to face up to the problem by trying to knock apart the triangle and free myself for action instead of worry." He spells out how he did it.

"First, I asked myself whether any of the triangle's three imponderables were really ponderable. I finally decided that the question, "What will competition do next?" was really something I should be able to figure out. After all, most industries are small worlds. We all have pretty much the same technical and marketing capabilities. Breakthroughs are rare. We all know, or think we know, the same major market needs.

"So I felt I should be able to forecast with reasonable accuracy—not 100%, but I don't need 100%—what my competitors were most likely to pull off under the circumstances of their market position,

267

availability of materials, and technical savvy. As soon as I got that side of the triangle squared away, I saw the real problem.

"The real problem is posed by the triangle's other two questions. These are areas I can't forecast nearly so well, based on what I think of as straight-line reasoning. I can't predict *when* competitors will come out with what they're capable of. And therefore I can't predict *what the effects might be* on my key accounts because this is largely, though not entirely, a factor of timing. So I invented a game that goes like this:

1. Think of the worst case first. Try to identify the single most unwelcome development that my two major competitors could come out with this year.
2. Try to define when they would be most likely to hit my territory with it and what its effects would be.
3. If the effects seem serious enough, devise a plan to limit their inroads or counteract them. If they don't seem that serious, forget them."

Regional and district managers in a wide range of industries have been discovering that facing up to the "When?" and "What effect?" aspects of the worst case they can make for competition helps clear the air and lets them feel more confident in their competitive frameworks. Managers' reactions are frequently concentrated on three points:

1. When the worst case is on the table, it sometimes doesn't seem so bad after all.
2. When it does seem bad, everyone knows it had better be dealt with.
3. By dealing with it, managers can often gain a countervailing advantage over competition that can turn the tables if the worst case comes to pass—or even keep it from occurring at all.

Some companies are teaching their managers worst-case planning as a regular part of management development. Here are some examples of what it's like in practice and how it can point the way to action.

A regional manager of an industrial engine transmissions marketer: "My worst case would be if our major competitor finally came out with an inexpensive transmission that we know he's been testing for the past three years. If he springs it on the market during the next two quarters—when price sensitivity is so acute and just after we've fallen on our faces with a new product introduction that failed—he could cause us huge problems. Our share of market would erode overnight, especially the matter of price.

"That would seriously threaten, maybe even end, our leadership. We'd suffer a major loss of distributor confidence, too. And I guess for the next three to five years it would pretty well obsolete our own new product strategy, which has been concentrated on the value end of the market, which accepts a premium price.

"What will I do? Sell like gangbusters while I still can, for one thing. Try to get a lock on the value market so we can have a stronghold somewhere if the bottom gets cut out from under us. Get to work with our distributors to show them how they can make more money by working with us—help them more to operate their own businesses better. And continue to bug our product development people to pay more attention to the low-end market and give me an entry in there that's not so overengineered and overcosted I can't sell it at a competitive price."

A regional manager of a building-supply manufacturer: "The worst case in my industry this year? That's easy. I live in fear of someone coming out with a cheap synthetic substitute for our basic insulated paneling. Everybody's been working on it since raw materials common to all of us fell into short supply. And the market is starved for something really new. The first ting a synthetic substitute would do is reduce our share of market and put a monumental squeeze on prices and profits. The second problem would be new competitors, who would flood the market and force out some of the majors, maybe even us.

"How can I face up to all this? Well, I don't have too many options. I can start now to stress the value of our present material and make sure the benefits are accepted by our major customers. I can set up fallback positions on pricing against the day when I will have to buy some of my market. I can even examine my product mix to see what else I can push to make up for future profit loss, possibly under conditions in which our existing materials won't be a part of our line any more."

A territory manager of a large manufacturer of health care products: "The worst case I'm living with is the specter of one of my major supermarket-chain customers going private-label in my largest-volume brand category. "If it comes this year, the timing couldn't be worse. We really need the cash flow to carry two new brands that haven't taken off yet but are burning up the promotion dollars. Maybe in a year or so it wouldn't be so bad. But now it could be a disaster. We might suffer a major wipeout of preferred shelf facings with our leading brand. Our sales would be hard hit.

"I think there are two things I can do, and I'm doing them. One is to generate every bit of consumer demand I can by plugging away with TV and in-store merchandising. I've got to show turnover. That may discourage the chain from going into competition with me, or maybe slow it down at least.

"Second, I'm putting together a new presentation to the chain's store managers and health care section managers to show them that our brand, in spite of higher price, still improves their profit more than a house brand would. Right now I'm running up a range of possible costs and prices for the private label so that I can plug the right ones into the presentation as soon as the product actually appears."

Worst-case planning, one district manager says, is like eating spinach: "I hate it. But I know it's good for me. So I do it." Another district sales manager has found that "facing up to what I fear most cuts my resistance to doing something about it." Perhaps one of the most interesting insights has come from a newly appointed manager. "Worst-case planning ought to become standard operating procedure for every manager. Once you prepare for the worst, the rest is easy. But what's the worst case about worst-case planning? That the things you fear the most won't happen and you'll do all that planning for nothing, right?

"Well, it isn't for nothing. What you learn about your competitors makes it worth the effort all by itself. The real bonus, however, is what you learn about *yourself:* what you're most afraid of and how well you can actually plan to combat your fears. That's got to make you a better manager. And anything that does that is worth whatever it costs."

What Should You Be Managing: Time, Territory, or the Growth of Your Customers?

Covering a territory is a matter of logistics. But does it mean covering everybody or covering customers whose contribution makes up most of the profits?

Regional sales manager: Key account concentration? Of course we're doing it. Our entire time- and territory-management system is geared to it. Why do you ask?

General sales manager: One of the reasons is that we're still calling it time and territory management. We're not really managing time; we're managing the allocation of our sales resources to secure our key accounts. Time is one consideration. So is capability: who sells to the account, who supports him. Then there's product mix, service, and all the rest. Why don't we think of it the way a customer does and call it something like resource management?

Regional SM: O.K., resource management. Our entire resource-management system is geared to key account concentration.

General SM: I have my doubts, but tell me about it.

Regional SM: We follow the 80-20 rule. The 20% of all our customers who give us up to 80% of our sales become our key accounts in the region. We concentrate a disproportionate amount of our time—oops, I mean resources—on them. Everybody else gets less. Isn't that what it's all about?

General SM: Not quite. How consistent are you in applying the 80-20 rule? Do you allocate 80% of your resources to the 20% of our customers who are the key accounts?

Regional SM: Maybe 60% or so would be more like it.

General SM: What do you do with the remaining 40%?

Regional SM: That goes to the B and C accounts, periodic purchasers who are giving us good business now but who need to be upgraded.

General SM: By applying the 80-20 rule again, what is the most likely percentage of them you think can be upgraded?

Regional SM: 20%?

General SM: Probably. So why does it take 40% of our resource allocation to have an effect on 20% of our minor customers?

Regional SM: That's not where all of it goes, you understand. A lot of that 40% is straight selling, picking up small orders, hitting the once-in-a-while customer.

General SM: How valuable is that for us?

Regional SM: Well, in some cases it makes the difference between a good quarter and a great quarter, sometimes even the difference between meeting budget and missing it.

General SM: How much of this marginal business would we lose if we cut back, say, by about 80%, on making personal calls to these accounts?

Regional SM: You want me to say about 20%?

General SM: I want you to say that we wouldn't lose anything, that we'd gain 20%.

Regional SM: By cutting back calls on marginals and light users?

General SM: No, by reallocating our resources toward our key accounts so that we could develop even more business from them, business that would more than make up for whatever we lost from minor customers.

Regional SM: Do you accept my estimate that we'd lose that business, though? Open the door to competition?

General SM: I accept it in part, and I'll tell you why in a minute. But even if you're right, do you accept my estimate that we could gain up to twice whatever we lose by redirecting our efforts onto our key accounts?

Regional SM: I don't know about up to twice. But more I'll agree with.

General SM: If you don't agree with up to twice, then you're only paying lip service to key account concentration. You really don't believe in it. That's what I meant when I said I have my doubts about how we're selling.

Regional SM: On the assumption that I believed in it according to your definition, why would I think we could gain up to twice what we'd lose?

General SM: Because of the very definition of a key account. You define it as a customer whose sales are key to us. I define it the other way around, from the customer's point of view as he looks at us. A key account by that definition is a customer to whom we as a supplier are vital. What does that perspective do to you?

Regional SM: It says that we may be leaving many of his needs unmet the present way we're serving him. If we're really vital to his success—and we must be if he already buys so much from us—then there may be other things we can sell him. That's theory. But what if the opposite is true? Suppose we've saturated him and don't know it?

General SM: What does saturation mean to you?

Regional SM: We've identified all his known needs. We're fulfilling them. Any other business with him could be marginal.

General SM: The key phrase in your answer is "known needs." The only saturation is in your knowledge of an account. You need to enlarge the surface area of your absorptive capacity to take in more information on his needs. The only thing worse than a saturated salesman is a saturated manager.

Regional SM: How do you suggest that I enlarge my needs awareness?

General SM: The first step is to open your mind to the possibility that more needs exist with our key accounts than we are currently meeting with our sales. The second step is to find out what they are and how we can fill them most profitably for both of us. The third step is to reallocate your resources away from lesser accounts and throw them against developing new key account business.

Regional SM: But what you're indicating is really developmental sales. That can be expensive, and it takes time before showing any results, if ever.

General SM: Isn't that just what you said you were doing right now with many of your nonkey customers—upgrading, I believe you called it? Isn't that developmental? Calling on prospects to develop them, calling on light useres, picking up a small order here and there to justify a call. That's mostly development work as far as I can see. All I'm doing is asking you to do your developing where the payoff has the greatest chance of being superior.

Regional SM: But how do I cover the waterfront?

General SM: Now you're right back to territory-management thinking again. I'm not asking you to cover a territory. I'm asking you to maximize its contribution to me in profitable sales revenues. I'm challenging you to decide how you want to do it: by covering everybody or by covering your key accounts like a blanket and finding new ways to do business with the rest.

Regional SM: How?

General SM: Telephone selling, for example. Direct mail. Seminars and conferences where a lot of the small customers come together in one place to meet with you, instead of us going all over creation to meet with them. Limiting personal calls to once a quarter. Computerizing standard repetitive orders, or at least automating them in some way. All of the above, and more.

Regional SM: There's an assumption that you're making in all of this, isn't there? That our competitors will play the game the same way. What if they don't? What if they cover the smaller accounts by personal selling compared to our trying to do business at a distance or only once in a blue moon? Won't they get the business?

General SM: Do we get business right now from these people just because we make personal calls on them?

Regional SM: Not enough, that's for sure.

General SM: So why assume that our competitors will? Even if they do, it will be just as epxensive for them in terms of cost per dollar of sales revenue as it is for us. And remember, the trade-off is that we're making more profitable sales with our key accounts. On balance, we win. And we should win big.

Regional SM: I have one more question. It has to do with our business of the future. How can we get in on the ground floor of new accounts or small growth companies if we follow your system?

General SM: I was hoping you'd get to that. Under what you're calling my system (in a few minutes, it's going to be your system, too), growth accounts are the exception to the rule. You're going to be encouraged to identify them, put together a portfolio of them, and overallocate resources to accelerate their growth. You'll be making bets on the future this way, so you have to choose them with care. If you're lucky, what percentage of them do you think will actually grow enough to become key accounts?

Regional SM: 20%?

General SM: I wonder how you knew that.

A Maximum of Participation May Go Hand in Hand with a Minimum of Profits

Market share or profits—or can the two ever be combined to get the best of both? And if not, is there an ideal ratio between them?

Sales representative: We're coming to the 120th day of our "Push the Profit Makers" plan. We've been following the plan closely, concentrating on the 20% of our products that give us 80% of our profits. Are you ready for a progress report?

Field sales manager (with trepidation): Sure.

Representative: Let's start with the good news. By pushing the big profit makers, we've stepped up their volume by about 12%. Our profit on sales is up over half that in our three main lines.

Manager (somewhat relieved): That's encouraging, to say the least.

Representative: There's more. We'll be paying more bonus dollars for the past quarter than we have for any similar period of our history. Naturally, it's our highest-performing salesmen who are earning them.

Manager: One swallow doesn't make a summer. I hope we can maintain that record for the next quarter.

Representative: With the momentum we'll have by then, we may do even better. Well, are you ready for the bad news now?

Manager: You mean there's a down side to all this?

Representative: Unfortunately so. While we're improving our penetration by our big profit makers, we're losing total participation with our key accounts. When we decided on our profit maker campaign, we said we'd have the ideal selling situation—a sales manager's dream, I think you called it. Our high performers would

275

be pushing our big-winner products to our heavy users. Do you remember, though, what your greatest fear was?

Manager: I wished we could predict the reactions of the heavy users.

Representative: Well, now we can. They've reacted. They're saying to us. "If that's the way you want to do business with us, on a big-winner basis, we'll go along with you. Why not? We appreciate the advantages of your concentration on a smaller line, the extra time we get from your best salesmen, the in-depth homework they're doing on applications and implementation. What we don't appreciate, though, is that you're no longer a full-line supplier to us."

Manager: And that's going to cost us. . . .

Representative: Just as you'd expect. If they can't do one-stop shopping with us, they're inviting our competitors in. *They're* eager to sell our customers the 80% of their needs while we zero in on the 20%.

Manager: But these are the products or applications we've analyzed as having only a marginal contribution to our profits—in some cases, a negative contribution. It was costing us to sell them.

Representative: The trouble is, what's unprofitable for us is profitable for some of our competitors. Actually, some find the business just as profitless as we do, but they're willing to buy it just to gain participation.

Manager: So you think that eventually they'll start buying our profit-making business.

Representative: Isn't that inevitable?

Manager: Not necessarily. There seem to be two options. One is to bring back 100% participation as our objective and return to the full-line, low-margin, and low-profit way of doing business. The other option is to improve our profits up front and cover our rear at the same time through high-penetration selling.

Representative: Suppose we take the high-penetration road. What do we do?

Manager: For starters, let's agree that we'll keep on, even intensify, our high-penetration policy. That will keep our stream of profits flowing strong. Next, let's divide our low-margin and no-margin products into two categories. First, those we can profit on by simply making them available at close to zero cost of sale. That means no promotional selling, no custom order taking, nothing but supply. This category may amount to 20% of the 80%. As for the products remaining in the second category, many of them can be bundled into systems with other product or services and sold as a team. That would give us a shot at premium pricing for the system and take the curse off the individual losers.

Representative: At most, that would rescue another 20% from oblivion—a total of 40% of the original 80%. Half isn't bad, but you know what management's going to ask us: What about the other half of our participation?

Manager: We'll continue to supply them, but only at prices profitable to us. That will probably discourage all but the most loyal customers. But if we can price profitably, why not pick up these marginal sources of income?

Representative: Now that you're down to the bottom of the barrel, I bet you've saved a more worthwhile idea for last.

Manager: Yes, and here it is: We make up our lost participation from profitless products with high-profit services to the customers who are cutting us out: services to help them cut the costs of their major functions, such as manufacturing and marketing.

Representative: We could end up with two major sources of profit: big profit-making products and big profit-making services. Would that make it easier to kiss off our lost participation?

Manager: Maybe not easier, but sweeter-tasting.